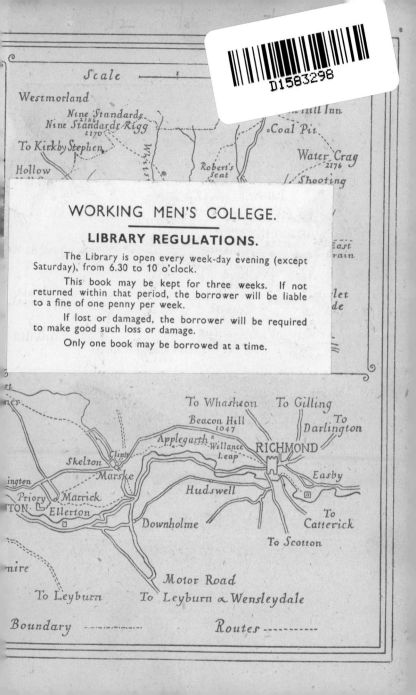

Scale

Westmorland

Nine Standards
Nine Standards Rigg 2170

To Kirkby Stephen

Hollow

Robert's Seat

Coal Pit

Water Crag 2176

Shooting

East

train

To Whashton   To Gilling

Beacon Hill
1047

Applegarth

To Darlington

Willance Leap

RICHMOND

Skelton   Clints
Marske

Easby

ington

Priory   Marrick
Ellerton

Hudswell

Downholme

To Catterick

To Scotton

nire

To Leyburn

Motor Road
To Leyburn & Wensleydale

Boundary ------

Routes ----------

SWALEDALE

East Gill Falls, Keld

SWALEDALE

by

ELLA PONTEFRACT

in collaboration with and with wood-engravings by

MARIE HARTLEY

LONDON

J. M. DENT & SONS LTD.

TO
OUR FRIENDS IN THE DALE

NOTE TO THE FIRST EDITION

WE have attempted in this book to give some idea of the history and scenery of Swaledale, and particularly to record the life of the people as we have known it for the last few years. Outside influence is coming quickly and customs are dying out, but the individual character of this remote English dale remains, and it is to be hoped that the beauty and grandeur of the country will not be spoilt.

We have together collected the material for the book, and wish to thank Mr. Ernest E. Taylor for his help and advice, Mr. E. R. Fawcett for some tales of the mining days, and many people in the dale for their recollections of old customs and events.

E. P., M. H.

1934.

NOTE TO THE FIFTH EDITION

It is now ten years since this book was written, and on reading it over we realize how many changes have taken place. Tan Hill coal-pit is no longer being worked. Muker Tup Show has been merged into the autumn fairs in Hawes; and its Agricultural Show has been suspended for the duration of the war. The ruins of Haverdale Mill have been pulled down and built into cottages. The War Department has extended its area; and the growing camp round Richmond has brought changes to the town. Here a renewed local pride has planned the restoration of the eighteenth-century theatre.

Edward R. Fawcett of Muker died in 1939. Thomas Lowis, the collector of antiques at Ivelet, has gone, and his treasures are dispersed. Richard Coates, lead-mining agent, of Fremington, died in 1937, and Susan Peacock of Tan Hill Inn in 1938. Almost all the lead-miners and many of the old 'standards' of Swaledale have gone. We regret that we can no longer talk to them of past and now almost forgotten things, but we cherish their memory, and are glad that their stories are recorded here.

E. P., M. H.

1944.

CONTENTS

LIST OF ILLUSTRATIONS

WOOD ENGRAVINGS

IN HALF-TONE

These are placed following page 88

MAPS AND PLAN

The Valley shut in by Fells

CHAPTER I

SWALEDALE

SWALEDALE in Yorkshire is a little country in itself. Once there, shut in by barriers of hills, you are satisfied: shrouded in its mystery, the rest of the world seems unimportant and unreal. You get this feeling in all the Yorkshire dales—those lovely valleys, each complete in itself, which start high up among the Pennines, and wind their way down to meet and mingle on the plain. But it is strongest in Swaledale, exaggerated perhaps by its remoteness, cut off by hills which are not single peaks but unbroken ranges. Wharfedale is within easy distance of the industrial area of the West Riding; a main road passes through Wensleydale on its way to the Lake District; but the road which curves and twists up Swaledale dwindles into a mountain pass which was a few years ago a rough track, but is now, alas! a tarred road.

You may enter it by this pass from Westmorland, by

lower roads from Wensleydale or Durham, or come straight up it, through Richmond, from Catterick or Darlington; but whichever way you enter, and in whatever season, you will feel its spell and be content. It is not, however, the contentment of stagnation which Swaledale gives, but the joy of adventure in a country which is ever changing. With each curve of the road there are new outlines to the hills, new becks and ravines to be discovered, new villages to surprise you suddenly over the brow of a hill.

This valley is unlike anywhere else in England. The springy turf, made up of innumerable wild flowers, on its meadows is reminiscent of the lower slopes of Swiss mountains, where the peasant women make hay of the short, rich herbage. The haymakers themselves, but for their gay caps and aprons, might be those peasants. The grey houses perched on the very edge of the fells have a suggestion of mountain huts about them. This Alpine character is especially felt on the lonely stretch between Keld and Muker, where the river, cut off from the rest of the valley by the hill of Kisdon, carves its way in falls and curves through one of the grandest pieces of country in England. Modern artificiality scarcely touches it. It is an English Tyrol, but with a character of its own. You never miss the snow-topped mountains there.

The dale starts on vast tracts of moorland, out of sight of cultivation or human dwellings. Then scanty pastures appear, and one or two gaunt houses with windswept trees beside them; the valley widens; grey hamlets cling to the hill; and a village huddles under it. Presently a church tower rises, and the villages come oftener, each one less perched and bleak than the last, until at Grinton is the first of those ancient buildings and ruins which occur so seldom in the higher reaches and so often in the lower. Then the country softens and woods appear, sometimes covering the whole hill-side, and attaining an exotic luxuriance in the secluded village of Marske—'smothered wi' trees,' as a daleswoman expressed it. And at the end there is the town of Richmond, with its ancient castle, its churches, its cobbled streets, its ruins, its glamour; and, a mile below it, all that is left of the monastery of white-cloaked monks, Easby Abbey, a fitting end to those thirty miles of grandeur.

Always, in the remotest places, you are conscious of the town of Richmond at the foot of the valley. Its cobbled streets, which have known nearly nine hundred years of civilization, offer relief if the open spaces become too over-powering, and human pride would see a little of the beauty man has wrought. You are conscious of it as those early settlers in the upper dale were conscious of it, knowing that there lay shelter from the raiding Picts and Scots. Hawes and Kirkby Stephen are nearer, and Hawes market is more used by the dalespeople; but the road down the valley leads to Richmond, and Richmond is still Swaledale. And in the town you are conscious of those roads to the hills. They call with their promise of adventure; and you cannot stay long in Richmond and not answer the call.

The river which gives its name to the dale rises high upon the hills which divide Yorkshire from Westmorland. It has an impetuous career, dancing down gullies, splashing as a waterfall over rocky ledges, cutting resolutely through gorges, bringing with it as it rushes down in flood great piles of stones, and leaving them on either side as a reminder that it can be a dangerous fellow when roused; until it flows in serener mood past Easby Abbey.

'The Swale is a right noble ryver,' said Leland, four hundred years ago.

'The Swale rusheth rather than runneth,' said Camden, a century later.

'Still Aire, swift Wharf, with Oze the most of might,

High Swale, unquiet Nidd, and troublous Skell,' said Spenser.

There have been other more recent writers who found this region terrifying in its upper parts, with no interest for the traveller except to hurry away from it as quickly as he could. To-day, we who think ourselves more enlightened will either love or dislike it. For there is one qualification needed to know and understand Swaledale, without which it may seem cold and grey; and that is a love of the hills. But in Swaledale they are called fells; pronounced 'faells.'

These fells shut the dale in, and you must love them in all their moods: on still days, when in a haze of blue they seem to sleep, and shadows make deep caverns on them; on boisterous days, when cloud shadows race across them like phantoms; on dull days, when a brooding sadness rests over them, the tragedy of all the years they have known; on stormy days, when one minute they are hard and pitiless, and the next lost and helpless behind a blizzard. In these and a hundred other moods you must love the fells or the dale is not for you. For even in the most sheltered, wooded part they are there, creeping down to the trees, the fields, the villages.

Grey fells, they are often called. But they are never lacking in colour. Heather creeps down from their summits as though a giant had tripped here and there as he strode from one top to another, spilling his paint of brown or green, purple or fawn, according to the season. Not all are topped with heather. In many the wiry grass creeps up to the summits, its summer greens changing to the browns of autumn till winter frosts bleach it to the shade of straw. Or the rushes get a hold, covering great stretches with their russet in the spring and later their claret-red flowers. Bracken reaches up them, here in patches, there just dappling the slopes, soft cinnamon in the winter, mingling with the green of the heather in summer, and blazing out a vivid rust in autumn.

Swaledale in the autumn is an unforgettable sight. Here is no gradual mingling of reds and golds, greens and browns and yellows, but each tree stands out detached, like a colour in a mosaic. In this riotous time of the turning of the leaves the trees have still the neatness of the moor about them. Of all the seasons, summer, flaunting her lavish greenery, has the least colour.

There is sound too on the fells; the angry clacking of grouse, the liquid pipe of curlews in the distance, the forlorn 'see-o-weet, see-o-weet,' as a plover swoops above, a metallic whirr of wings as a snipe flies suddenly downwards, the anxious call of sheep and lambs. And through all there is the sound of the wind—wind running with soughing noises along the grass and rushes, and with moans among the rocks, rustling through the heather, whistling round the scars, and howling along the summits.

After storms the fells are a network of peaty streamlets trickling down to the river below, and appear like a relief-map. Seeing them so, you realize how they have made the river what it is. Knowing them too, you realize the fitness of the grey cottages built from their rocks and stones; and perhaps come nearer to understanding the stoical independence and individuality of the people who live in them, shut in to themselves by the fells. Like the dwellers in Mr. H. G. Wells's *Country of the Blind*, imprisoned by high mountains, they have developed those characteristics which their lives needed. In these days of people cut to a pattern their originality is refreshing. There are 'characters' still in Swaledale, but chiefly among the older people, to whom distance is still distance. Cars are coming, more and more every year. Wireless has come. The younger ones are being moulded like the rest of the world. As a daleswoman put it: 'We're a deeal mair in amang't these last twenty years.'

They are a spare, virile people, showing in their handsome faces, waving hair, and dignified bearing signs of their Scandinavian forefathers who settled in these parts. They have inherited traits which are inherent in the Norwegians —courtesy, and natural manners, and a willingness to help each other. The early Norse settlers gave the villages their names, from which many of the names of the people are taken.

There is something of tragedy, too, in this remote valley. An industry grew up here, flourished for generations, had a wave of great prosperity, and then died. Rich veins of lead run in a wide belt across its hills and the hills of Wensleydale. It is known that these were worked extensively by the Romans. Some years ago a miner at Hurst broke through into an old working and found a pig of lead weighing about a hundred and seventy pounds, stamped with the inscription: 'ADRIAN' (117-138). This was supposed to be in the British Museum, but cannot now be traced. The Romans used native labour in the mines, and are thought to have had a garrison from which their soldiers kept the Brigantine miners in order. Their own convicts were also employed in them. But the mines were there before the Romans. It is thought that the mineral wealth of Britain was one of their reasons for conquering the country. Many of the Roman cathedrals were roofed with lead from their British mines.

Little is known of the early diggers, but they have left their traces in the thrown-out heaps, covered now with turf and heather in contrast with the bareness of more recent tippings. Later workers, knowing nothing of their predecessors, christened them 't' owd man,' as one person. Sometimes a miner would start on a vein of lead, and find that in a yard or so it gave out, the earlier miners having worked it from the other end. 'T' owd man's gitten in,' he would call out to his fellows. The track of 't' owd man' can be followed over the hills.

During the twelfth and thirteenth centuries, the great period of church and abbey building in England, much lead was used for roofing, and the industry developed. There is a record of the lead merchants of Richmond in the twelfth century. The seventeenth century was another period of expansion. At this time many of the mines were owned by the Wharton family, though a few were still held by the Crown. In the eighteenth and early nineteenth centuries the trade flourished, and fortunes were made. More and more levels were opened, and houses were in great demand. In a tiny cottage on the fells near Marske a man and his wife lived with their seventeen children and five lodgers who worked in the mines close by. Theirs was quite a typical example. The paths striking at all angles up the fells led to the various shafts and levels. Along them too the ore was carried to the smelting-mills, and the smelted lead was taken on pack-horses to Richmond and Barnard Castle.

About 1860 a change came. Spanish lead, owing to its greater proportion of silver, could be bought cheaper. The Swaledale veins went deeper and deeper into the hills, making them more expensive to work. And there was the difficulty of transport. One mine after another closed down, and the miners went into Durham and Lancashire to find work. Their ruined cottages testify to their numbers, though time has softened the tragedy of their going.

There are those who say that the closing of the mines was a good thing; that there are far too many graves of that period in the churchyards of men in their forties who died from the effects of lead-poisoning. Others, and among them some of the old miners, have a reverent love for the mines, an unconscious appreciation of the romance of digging

metal from the earth, and a fanatical desire to see them working again. One old miner declared that there was no more
beautiful sight in the world than the hot, white metal as it
was poured from the smelting-baths into the moulds.
'Visitors,' he said, emphatically, 'would come by hundreds
to see it, if only the mines were being worked again.' He
knew all the shafts and levels by heart, knew them so well
that he could go into the hill at the Old Gang mines and
come out again at Arkengarthdale, four miles away. This
man's father had been a blacksmith at the mines, where he
made not only horseshoes but moulds for the lead, and
many of the tools.

It is only within the last few years that some of the villages have lost the dilapidated air which the ruined buildings
gave them. Holidaymakers have done their part towards
this. Tourists have brought money to the dale, either as
visitors or by buying and repairing a ruin for a country
cottage. Only in a few less fortunately placed villages is the
feeling of desolation left.

The remaining people adjusted themselves to the new
conditions. Mining had never been a whole-time job. In
those days of bad ventilation the men could not stay underground for more than a certain time. Some of them had
worked small shafts of their own in their spare hours,
sorting out the ore and smelting it in pots in the garden;
others had small-holdings, which they farmed. As the out-
of-work men left the district numbers of these small-
holdings were thrown together to make bigger farms, and
these were rented by the miners who would not leave the
dale. The thrifty ones, having at the later period of the
industry made good wages, had saved considerable sums of
money. Buildings which had housed three or four families
were made into one good house; cottages which were not
needed were used as barns; and the people settled down to a

new life and a new outlook. A few of the men who remained took up fresh work. One miner, who rented a
small-holding at Skeugh Head, near Keld, became a
butcher. Twice a week he killed and cut up a sheep, and
carried it in a large basket on his head up and down the dale
to sell. Once a year, for Thwaite Fair in October, he killed
a cow. Before this, the only butcher came over the moors
from Askrigg in Wensleydale once a week.

The new farmers turned their attention, as the ones
already established had long done, to sheep-rearing. To-day,
nearly every man has to do with sheep-farming, and his
thoughts and conversation are of sheep. Other farmers have
their grain and root-crops, but these upland farmers have
only sheep. They keep a few cows, partly to get manure for
the hayfields, and one or two pigs to feed the family and
extra help during hay-time, the hay being used to feed the
stock in the winter. The moorland farms are measured by
the few acres of pastures surrounding them, but each has
grazing for sheep on the moors. From the moment when the
first lambs appear, through shearing and dipping, and the
excitement of the local shows and sales, to the final oily
dipping as a protection against winter storms, the farmer's
work is largely with the sheep. And when winter sets in
there is the constant watchfulness, and the tedious carrying-
up of hay to the moors if it is frosty or snowy.

Not often at any time of the year do you look up to the
fells without seeing a solitary figure silhouetted against the
sky, outlined on the lower slopes, or merging into the higher
slopes as he climbs or descends from rounding up the sheep.
Wet or fine the shepherd is out. A sunny day after rain will
see rows of sodden coats and breeches hanging out to dry
at every farm-house. But it is a fine life. As the shepherds
come down from the fells with the rolling gait they develop,
theirs seems the kind of life man was meant to live.

We once found, on the steep, grassy slope above Hoggarth's Bridge, a miniature plan of the countryside, evidently made by children from a near-by farm. Brown pebbles made the walls of the fields, in small squares on the lower slopes, bigger and more curious in shape as they rose, and ending abruptly as they were supposed to reach the open moor. A tiny round of stones represented a sheep-pen, and twigs made the troughs. The lambs were white pebbles, and the sheep fir-cones. How like a sheep as it bends to eat a fir-cone is! The narrow end is the head, that rather insignificant part of a sheep; the rest is the body with its heavy wool reaching to the ground. The cones were huddled thickly round the troughs, and dotted on what were supposed to be the fells, most of them with one or a pair of white pebbles beside them. The childish builders had grasped and given out the very essence of this countryside to-day. It was like the work of some primitive artist.

This picture is worth remembering while exploring the dale. It will help you to understand it and its people better. Theirs is not the dull life which is sometimes imagined. We think of one man leaning up against the porch of the cottage in which he lives alone, far from another house, his scanty pastures forming a ring round him, the rest open fells; and talking with pride of his sheep, telling how all of them were different. 'Nay,' he said, 'I nivver count t' sheep. I ken if yan's missing. How? Why a sheep's as different as fooak; thar's nivver tweea t' seeame i' a flock.'

The dale has given its name to the kind of mountain sheep which graze on its fells, pedigree Swaledales which are widely kept in many upland districts. They are small, neat sheep with black heads and legs, and if their wool is not as thick and fine as that of lowland sheep, they can exist all the year round in bleak, exposed places which would soon kill

off the larger varieties. There are cross-breeds now in the
dale, but they are kept to the lower pastures.

The fells themselves would seem lonelier without the
sheep. And yet the fells were there before the sheep, before
the mines, before men thought it possible to live among
them. On all these changes they have gazed, giving up to the
people their mineral wealth, and feeding their flocks. Some
of the early dwellers amongst them gave them their names,
Lovely Seat, Great Shunnor Fell, Water Crag, Rogan's
Seat, Kisdon, Harkerside. What better adventure than to
explore them, to discover their ravines and valleys, to follow
the paths which cross them, the old pack-horse tracks along
their sides; to follow too that winding road down the valley
from where it slips away into Westmorland to where the
dale joins the plain?

Keld

CHAPTER II

KELD

KELD is the last and highest village in Swaledale, a goal to be reached from the valley, a haven to come down to from the hills. There are farms and hamlets beyond it, but the real life of the dale stops there. It is a metropolis for the head of the dale, and it is conscious and proud of its importance. It has the last shops, the last chapels, the last school and village hall. And the bus from Richmond turns back there. The mention of Keld brings to mind the grey village nestling in its hollow; but it brings back also the whole dale, the fells, the river, the people. For here is the essence of the upper dale.

The Vikings who founded and settled in this hollow chose their site well. Here they could live sheltered and safe, for raiders sweeping down from the north would see nothing of the hidden settlement just off their line of march. Its secluded position is still a great advantage, for the merely passing tourist never finds it. Those who keep along the road to the boundary and Westmorland see only a high, gaunt shooting-lodge, a shop, a cottage, and a Wesleyan chapel, comparative new-comers. This is known as Keld Green. To discover the village you must take the road which drops down into it by the War Memorial and, but for a rough lane, ends there. For all these things, and because it is the last place where accommodation can be had, we have made Keld a centre from which to explore the head of the dale.

There are three places at which you can stay. The Cat Hole Inn stands at the top of the hill like a sentinel guarding the way to the village, for an inn must consider passers-by more than its own comfort. The wind-swept building is seen from far down the valley, from the Buttertubs Pass, unexpectedly from bends on the roads to Tan Hill and Kirkby Stephen. The original inn, which stood lower down the hillside, is now a barn. There have been many explanations of its name, but the most generally accepted is that the neighbourhood was once the haunt of wild cats. During the mining boom the name was changed to 'The Miners' Arms,' but happily it went back to the old one.

Butt House, on the road down to the village, is another good house at which to stay. It is also the post office and village shop, a convenient arrangement. The shop is very small, three customers make it congested, but it is an instance of how much can go into little room. You can generally get what you ask for. Park Lodge, a roomy house at the end of the village, is the third. It has a genial landlady, and the music of the river and the falls is never silent there.

An isolated cottage up a road on the left is called 'Starling Castle.' Many of the houses in Swaledale are 'castles' or 'halls,' as befits their independent owners. Is not 'Starling Castle' an inspiration? It is very tiny, and has no land, but a man can be excused for calling his house a castle if he puts a modest starling before it. Below it the village seems to draw up in welcome, and the chapel manse juts cheerily out into the road.

The Congregational Chapel on to which the manse is built has had a changeable history. It was a chapel in very early times, but its origin is uncertain. It has been an Anglican church—Leland mentions it in 1540—but it was closed, probably when the church at Muker was built in 1580, and fell into ruin. In a churchwarden account of 1695 this entry occurs: 'For walling up Keld Chapel door, £0 1s. 0d.' In 1745 it was restored as a Calvinistic place of worship, but in 1789 it was again in a ruinous state when a man named Edward Stillman, an Independent, arrived in Keld. For two years he had wandered about Upper Swaledale preaching in barns. When he came to the ruins at Keld he declared that there he would build his chapel and preach the gospel. He is chiefly remembered for his remarkable walk to London, on which he spent sixpence, and begged £700 to rebuild the chapel and house. His long, hard ministry lasted forty-eight years.

The windows in Keld chapel are clear and look on to the fells. In the homely building, listening to the simple service, life seems to lose most of its complications. The great day at the chapel is the Sunday School Anniversary day. Then whole families arrive; the mother, proud and triumphant, carrying the baby, and followed by the rest of the children, the father behind them, a little shamefaced and uncomfortable in his Sunday suit. They fill every corner. And the school-children, in new frocks and hats, sit in front, facing the congregation, and recite. For an hour you might have gone back quite a generation.

There is no church at Keld. The nearest is at Muker, five miles away. That and the absence of a big house give it a communal feeling, refreshing to come across in England. There is no class distinction amongst the farmers, owning or renting their farms. The hired boy is often the son of another farmer who has more sons than he needs at home. The lack of a big house has produced in the people a degree of independence which perhaps makes them a little hard. But it has produced also a naturalness uninfluenced by social distinctions, so that there is no servility, but an open friendliness once their first shyness is overcome. They are not curious about strangers, finding them interesting only so far as they affect their own lives, and being unable to visualize an existence different from the one they know.

The problem of finding work for their sons is a big one for the dale farmers. At some seasons they could do with them all on the farm, but at others there is not enough work. A generation ago, before the North Riding County Council took them over, the farmers kept up the roads, each one undertaking a certain length; and this provided extra work and pay for their sons. Very different roads they must have been in those days, for the farmer merely took stone from the moor, broke it up, spread it thickly, and left it to be smoothed down gradually by carts and traps.

The village school is opposite the chapel. At ten to nine in the morning during term time there is a sudden shouting and a clanging of clogs, and a straggling procession appears over the hill. Starting at the point where the children come to Keld rather than to Muker, it has been added to from farms and hamlets on the way; a noisy, rather reluctant procession, big sisters dragging unwilling small brothers by the arm. Later, the children come into the road to play and drill, another advantage of a road which goes to nowhere. 'As big as you can.' 'As small as you can.' 'As wide as you can,' the teacher's voice calls out, and the prospective sheep-farmers stretch on tiptoe, crouch down, and spread out their arms in turn. They are sturdy children, with an easy, natural air, and a doggedness gained from grappling with all weathers on their journeys. They have their sense of fun, if it is a little grim. Once we left a walking-stick wedged in the grass at the roadside, and coming back an hour or two later, found it in the same place with a magnificent nettle tied to the handle.

Cottages turn off at all angles as the road runs down to the gravel-covered square which has taken the place of the village green. The old houses gaze on the innovation unconcerned, not realizing the loss, and the village hall stands imposingly beside them. In the cottage below the hall lived Richard Alderson, known as Neddy Dick, who was famous for his 'musical stones.' These he had collected from the Swale, and he played tunes on them with two wooden sticks. Since his death the cottage has been enlarged.

The hall at Keld seems big enough to swallow the whole village. One sometimes longs to see the green again without its lofty walls, until one realizes what the hall means to the people at the remote head of the dale. Here their concerts, dances, and meetings are held; here they even have a badminton club. Its walls are part of their past also, for the smooth stones of the front were brought from a disused smelt-mill up the West Stonesdale Beck. Occasionally a travelling draper comes to display his goods, hiring the hall for a day. His chief mode of advertising is to allow the school-children in during their playtime. They run round the room, their clogs thundering on the wooden floor; then they go home and tell their mothers all about it. Darlington, the nearest large town, is still a long and expensive journey, and the draper does a good trade. His biggest stock consists of aprons of all patterns and colours. The women are hardly ever without their aprons; tidying themselves up means putting on a clean one. A corner even pokes up above their coats when they start out to spend a few days with a relative in some other part of the dale. Nowadays the small girls wear aprons like their mothers, but forty or fifty years ago the children wore white pinafores over turkey-red cotton dresses. 'An' nice an' bright they leuked,' one woman who remembers them says.

Twice a year the people make some effort to pay for the upkeep of the village hall. In the spring they have what they call a 'May Stir,' and at the beginning of November an 'Autumn Stir,' generally a concert with a supper and dance to follow. The local women do the catering. For a week beforehand delicious smells waft out of cottage doors, and you find the women, busy and rather heated, rolling and beating, and opening oven doors. They count in stones, not dozens. One will promise to make up a stone of flour into tarts, another into cakes, another into bread. There is something delightfully natural about it all, a communal idea which spreads the interest. Those who have promised to bake call in one or two other women to help, so that for many the excitement of the event begins a week before.

Keld Sports, perhaps a bigger 'stir,' are another occasion for much baking. They are held in June at Rowley Bottom, a field below West Stonesdale, about half a mile above Keld. There is a true local spirit about them. The field slopes down on either side to the beck, and the people sit on one bank to watch the sheep-dog trials on the other. These were an innovation in 1932, and some competitors from afar, whose dogs were used to cut-and-dried courses and went astray on the wrong side of the stream, declared bitterly that it was not a trial but an impossibility. The village band plays at intervals, between which the bandsmen enter for quoits and races. The band-master has difficulty in getting them together again for the next burst of music, a round of quoits being too important to be interrupted.

The local boys do not come off badly against outsiders in the sports, and they fit into the picture better. We can think of one tall, well-made youth with fair, curly hair pushed back from his face, looking, as he took the pole jump, like one of his Viking ancestors. There are races for the children. The two men who were managing them got muddled over size and age. An athletic girl in a white dress won the race for her own age so easily that instead of giving her the prize they moved her into the next class. Public opinion, however, was with her, and the crowd shouted, 'Go it, li'le white 'in!' and cheered as she ran. She won. She was a determined child.

But the tea tent is the chief glory. Here is all the bread and cake and pastry. And here are the women, still busy, filling up plates and passing tea, and watching that nobody slips away without paying. Great plates of pastry disappear like magic. The old farmer next to us had no time for conversation; his right hand moved forward for another piece while his left held the remains of the last.

Nearly every village in the dale has its band, usually a good one. The practices are held in a room in the village, often an old cottage with the words BAND ROOM painted above the doorway. There are private practices too. Sometimes as you pass a barn in Angram, a mile below Keld, the noise of a trumpet sounds terrifyingly through its walls.

The name Keld, given to it by Norse settlers, is from the Scandinavian *kelda*, a spring or stream. But only the sound of the stream from which its name sprang reaches the village. Coming down the winding street it seems unbelievable that between the village and the fells there is a deep gorge with the river foaming at the bottom, grinding at the precipice on which the cottages stand. At a period before the Ice Age, the river flowed round the west side of the hill of Kisdon to Muker, and there would be no break in the fell behind the village. But probably in some great flood the water cut a way through a fault in the strata, the river turned down this, and deposit gradually filled up the old bed. The struggles of the Swale through its new channel have resulted in some of the finest waterfalls in England.

A rough flight of steps down the cliff below Park Lodge leads to Catrake Falls. These falls come over curving ridges of rock into a dusky pool, sometimes as gentle cascades, catching in their fall a glint of sun through the trees; sometimes as raging torrents, dyed a deep brown by the peat, rushing to clutch and destroy anything they can reach, the pool a whirlpool, its edges thick with yellow foam. It is awe-inspiring so, but it is loveliest when, its first fury past, the water comes over in an exquisite transparency which is neither green nor brown, but a mixture of each; the wine of the moor pouring down into the valley. An opening on the Keld side of the falls is an entrance to a lead-mine, the Sir George Denys level, which was designed to run three miles underground to Lonin End where the Swale begins. It was the first long level to be made, and was a failure, as the ore was soon exhausted.

The river flowing in its chasm through Keld is magnificent, but it is a thing to itself, not a part of the community as is Kisdon. This isolated hill dominates the valley between Keld and Muker, and helps to make the curves and bends which are characteristic. Kisdon is so much a part of Keld that sometimes you are inclined to take it for granted, and forget how all the loveliest features of the fells are gathered together upon it. Its heather-topped summit, a darker patch among the surrounding hills, tells from far away where the village lies. Wild flowers fill its lower meadows—splashes of marsh marigolds, sheets of buttercups; bluebells and wood anemones creep up to the wild orchis and the mountain cranesbill; and yellow and purple pansies in their turn spread gaily up to the heather. Now a patch of woodland is enclosed by crumbling walls, now juniper trees crouch like dwarfs upon it, now it breaks out in limestone scars. Over it long centuries ago the funeral processions passed, along a track known as the Corpse Way, because it was the route taken in medieval days to the nearest consecrated burial ground twelve miles away. We shall tell the story of it in the chapter on Grinton. On its way up Kisdon it passes a deserted farm-house which stands black and dreary against the hill, its empty windows looking tragically down the valley. Some years ago the land beneath this house cracked, and the people were afraid to stay. In its desertion it adds to the fascination of the hill.

The name Kisdon is derived from the Celtic *kis*, little, and *dun*, a detached hill. After the channel of the Swale was diverted to its north side it was probably an island for a time. Except for the strip of land on which Keld stands it is an island to-day, having the Swale on its north and east sides, Skeb Skeugh Beck on the west, and Muker Beck on the south. On Jeffrey's Map of Yorkshire, 1771, it is called 'Kisdon Island.'

Pure mountain air flows down to Keld from the surrounding fells. Having breathed it for a few minutes you unconsciously stand straighter. Walking is easy in that atmosphere, even over rough moors, and on the short turf you feel to be carried along.

Becks' Meeting

CHAPTER III

THE SOURCE OF THE RIVER AND DALEHEAD

THE road which runs from Keld into Westmorland has a determined air. 'Come along, come along,' it seems to say; 'but don't expect to find me easy. It's a serious business, this getting from one county to another. But follow me, and I'll show you where the river starts.'

It is exciting to go in search of a river's source. Too often we see our English rivers only as broad waterways. But, having tracked one to its beginnings, seen its first, feèble struggles, and followed it step by step until it grows up, you have a very different feeling about it. It is a friend compared with a mere acquaintance. The road to Kirkby Stephen knows what it is about when it calls you to follow it and find adventure among the high fells which roll backwards from Keld.

Like many other roads in the dale, this ancient track, along which pedlars travelled between the two counties, has developed into a negotiable motor road. Doggedly and courageously it goes, now mounting the fell, now running round it to avoid a hill, surmounting obstacles simply, perhaps a little crudely, as befits its primitive beginnings; a persistent mountain pass, finding the quickest way to the border.

If you would climb the hill and find the source of the river, there is no time to linger; meanderings are for a less ambitious journey. On this expedition even the waterfalls must be just one of the many beauties which crowd upon you at every step, making a glorious whole. The fells rise sheer above the road, their sparse meadowland growing less and less until the heather and the bilberries conquer it, climbing down in their triumph over the wall which would hold them back; until they in their turn give way to the wiry, moorland grass higher up. Hoggarth's Bridge, where the road turns sharply and leaves the river, is the last road bridge of the Swale. The river flows more restrainedly here, as if it remembers guiltily the havoc which its exuberance once caused. Even the waterfall hides under the trees below the bridge, though betrayed by its restless voice.

In the year 1899 there was a cloudburst on Shunnor Fell, and volumes of water rushed down Great Ash Gill behind Hoggarth's. The people in the farm-house at the foot of the ravine had just time to escape through the bedroom windows, but the house was a ruin when the water subsided, and it has not been rebuilt. The flood joined the already overflowing Swale, and tore down the valley, clutching angrily at everything which came its way; sheep, hens, dogs, buildings were picked up like matchwood, and most of the bridges were washed away. The farm-house sheltering behind fir-trees at the top of the hill by the roadside was built in this very different situation to replace the ruin on the ravine.

The road mounts upwards, leaving the river far below. It

passes a farm-house, a ruin beside the road—once itself a farm known as Crook Seat—a pasture surrounded by black walls, a round sheep-pen upon whose sod-covered walls cotton flowers wave silky plumes, a stack of bracken thatched with rushes; then the walls end, and there is nothing but moorland, the road, and rough posts to mark it. Plovers call forlornly overhead; the metallic whistle of a curlew ends in a trill far away. Sheep have cropped the grass at the edges of the road, and here in spring the plovers bring their young ones out for exercise; fluffy, brown balls, very wobbly on their legs, which when frightened crouch into the grass and heather, and are almost indistinguishable from them. Tit-larks are numerous here, and seem friendly and companion-able after the other moor birds. They make their nests in the earthy banks at the side of the road, and will dart out from them if frightened, giving away the secret of their small, brown eggs. You hear the piteous cry of a lamb which has lost its mother, the anxious answer of a sheep, and the sudden silence as they find each other; or the puzzled bleat of a sheep calling for a lamb which will never answer its call.

Suddenly, in the heart of the fells the stream trickles by the road again, called the River Swale no longer, but Birk-dale Beck. It seems to caress and soften the grim moor. Glad to have started on its journey, it calls other becks to join it; the place where Crooked Sike Beck, flowing down from Coldbergh Edge on Nine Standards Rigg, joins it is known as Becks' Meeting. At one time Crooked Sike Beck flowed across the road, and had to be forded; later the road was raised to bridge it.

Presently the ravine of Uldale is seen to the left, cutting into the hill almost at right angles to the road. It is at the top of Uldale that the beck first makes its way silently under flattened grass, flowing quicker as the land drops, and collecting a stone or two, until, growing with every yard, it can call itself a stream, and the source of a great river.

Near the top of the pass the hills seem to part to make a way through, the grass verge widens, the brown posts change to black-and-white ones, and the road seems to stop and rest, as though its hardest work were finished; slipping down the hill to Nateby and Kirkby Stephen is play after what lies behind. Two stones mark the boundary of Yorkshire and Westmorland, with a space between them which both counties claim. The road on this stretch is well kept, for, having claimed it, both counties mend it. The land round the boundary is marked on maps as Lamps Moss, surely a mistake for Lambs Moss. The name probably arose from the prevalence of a bright, green moss which is plentiful on some parts of the fells in early spring, and is looked for eagerly by the farmers, as it provides feed for the sheep before the grass begins to grow. A man lower down the dale is known as 'Mosser' because the sheep he shepherded grazed on a mossy patch of moor. His son gets the name of 'Young Mosser.'

An old, inscribed stone known as Hollow Mill Cross which once stood at the border here is marked as a cross in maps as early as the sixteenth century. There is a tale of a pedlar who, in 1664, while travelling from Askrigg, up Swaledale, and over the border to his home in Kirkby Stephen, carrying money received for the goods he had sold, was murdered near this cross. Although a farmer was suspected of the crime, strong enough evidence could not be produced to condemn him. Two men questioned at York Castle in 1666 told how, going on to the moor to fetch two young horses, they were parted, and one heard the sound of a blow, and a voice cry 'Murder!' Later he saw in the gill near Hollow Mill two men with their backs towards him, and a bundle on the ground in front of them. Some months after they were in the same place looking for horses, and found bones and the skull of a man in the gill. A gruesome happening in this wild place.

Suddenly, as you near the ridge, the valley of the Eden appears far below, green and luxuriant, patched with corn-fields and dark woodland. Villages rest very comfortably on that level vale; a white cottage shines out, and a farm-house with stacks and out-buildings around it. A train, seeming from this distance to crawl, leaves a trail of smoke across the plain. To the north and east beyond Stainmore are the heights of Mickle Fell and Warcop Fell, while far off to the west rises the jagged line of the Lake District moun-tains. If it is clear they can be picked out—Skiddaw and Saddleback, and the crags of Scawfell and Scawfell Pike with the ridge of Mickledore between them. It is best to be there early to see these mountains clearly; being in the west, they haze over as the day advances.

Life in the sheltered Eden valley must be pleasant, giving a good return for labour on the land. The view of it jostles in your mind with that of the moorland valley behind, where life is not so easy.

The two ridges which shut in the last stretch of Swaledale end just beyond the boundary; on the right Nine Standards Rigg, 2,170 ft., is famous for nine stone pillars reared on its edge, but not seen from here; and on the left High Seat rising up from the rest of the ridge in a flat-topped summit, 2,326 ft., the source of four rivers, is the Swale, the Ure, the Cotter, and the Eden.

The best way to climb High Seat is to leave the road a little below Hollow Mill Cross, and then cut across the moor, making for the top cairns. But in Swaledale one does not call the heaps of stones which mark the tops 'cairns,' but 'curracks' or 'stone men.' A sense of direction is an asset here, for there are few tracks, rails, or posts to mark the way as on the Lake District fells. A good map is essential; and climbs attempted in mist bring little reward. It is heavy going; there are bogs or peat crevasses to avoid or plough through, and ridges of grass or heather over which to stumble. Here and there in the rough grass you find the fragile flowers of the grass of Parnassus. It is about an hour's climb to the summit.

The view from the top is like the one below, but here, as on all heights, you feel the nearness of the hills around. More of Mallerstang, the lonely dale which forms the upper part of Edendale, is seen, and across it to the west the peak of Wild Boar Fell. Against the sinking sun, unrelieved by light and shade, the hills might be settings on a stage. The valley with the white road winding up it seems painted too. Above it are the crags of Mallerstang Edge, where peregrine falcons still breed.

The boundary of Yorkshire and Westmorland cuts across Nine Standards Rigg and High Seat, and down through Hell Gill into Mallerstang. This boundary marks the end of several estates, the owners of which used to ride their bounds every ten years. Following the ridge of High Seat to the peak of Lady's Pillar, there is on the currack which marks its summit a stone carved with the initials A P and the date 1664. When she was staying at Pendragon Castle in Mallerstang Lady Anne Clifford had these cut to mark the bounds of her manor. In 1890 Captain Frederick Horner Lyell, a later lord of the manor, carved his initials on another side of the currack. The local name for Lady's Pillar is Lady Building, pronounced 'beelden,' but few of the dalespeople have seen or heard of the stone. 'It were before our time,' they will say, with an incapacity to comprehend an existence before their grandfathers' day. None of their grandfathers had ridden the bounds in Lady Anne Clifford's day, so there is an end to it.

Descending Lady's Pillar on the Mallerstang side, keeping to the right bank of Hell Gill but on the top of the ravine, at the point where it is steepest, there is an inscribed stone, known as the 'Jew Stone.' It originally stood six feet high, but some workmen who were laying the railway track through Mallerstang climbed up to find it, and because they could not read the inscription, broke the stone. Now the pieces sink into the grass and are difficult to find. A man locally called a Jew because of his long beard followed the Eden from the sea to its source and carved the inscription, part of which is in Latin and part in Greek. The translation reads:

(Latin) William Mounsey, a lone traveller, having undertaken a journey at the mouth of the Eden as far as the source, and having finished it pays his bows to its genius and nymphs. March 15th, 1850. (Greek) Seek the river of the soul whence it sprung, when thou hast served the body in a certain order—when thou hast acknowledged thy duty in the sacred Scriptures—thou shalt be raised again to the order from which thou art fallen. Let us fly with ships into our dear native land; for we have a native land whence we have come, and our Father is there.

✡   ⌐L

The path beyond the stone leads down Hell Gill to Aisgill Cottages in Mallerstang, just above which the Eden takes its sudden turn into Westmorland.

The descent from Lady's Pillar into Swaledale can be made down Great Sleddale or over the fell to Angram. But from High Seat it is best to follow Little Sleddale, whose stream, with never a cottage or farm to grace it, creeps stealthily down to join Birkdale Beck. Even here, where it gathers in the Little Sleddale Beck, Birkdale is a lusty fellow, babbling noisily of the way it has come, and drawing back now and again in awe at the sombre valley it has entered. Birkdale gives the Swale its season of youthful pessimism; nothing breaks the starkness of the hills on either side; nor does the first farm-house, Ellers, dispel the gloom and desolation, but rather seems to rise defiantly on the hill-side, ever on the defensive against the weather and its grim surroundings. Near it two trees wave protesting arms. A lane climbs behind it to the Kirkby Stephen road.

Below Ellers the valley widens, the sunlight creeps in again, and Birkdale Beck rushes joyfully to meet Great Sleddale Beck from the next valley. Here where they meet at Lonin End the Swale begins. Lonin comes from the Old English *loan*, a lane; the word is still used locally. This lane ends in a ford across the Birkdale Beck, and led to the mine which the long level near the Catrake Falls in Keld was intended to reach. At this junction which makes the Swale there seems to be a little of everything which is found in the valley: the fells, a few meadows with a stone barn, a ford, a sheep-fold, the remains of a mine. It is as though the whole life of the dale sprang up here with the start of the river.

Great Sleddale is an excellent route by which to climb or descend from Great Shunnor Fell. Far up it there is an old copper-mine, now deserted. It is said that there are rich veins of copper in the hill yet, and many men have spent their savings in trying to work it. There is a story of its being leased to a Reeth man who put two men to work there. In a little while they struck a vein, and one man went on with the digging while the other walked the fourteen miles to Reeth to fetch his employer and tell him the good news. It was before the days of buses, and they hired a horse and cart in which to drive back. The double journey took several hours, and when they arrived the man had just reached the end of the vein. But men still hope, and no doubt it will be tried again.

A little lower than Lonin End is Stone House, a prosperous-looking farm-house opening on to a flagged yard; from it a path runs to its neighbour, The Firs, a cosy house, older and less altered than most in the dale, and with a whitewashed porch like a dairy; on its window-sill a white cat usually dozes. At one time somebody must have brought a white cat into the dale, and now nearly all the cats are white; they seem to have exterminated the other species like the grey squirrels have the red in some parts of England.

The narrow valley of Dalehead, far from a road and shut in by fells, seems to us the nearest approach on land to a desert island. The kitchen at The Firs fits in with the picture. To step into it is to experience a feeling of completeness. Here are the essentials of everyday life, neatly stored in shelves and corners, not pushed away out of sight. Between the old beams on the ceiling wooden shelves are slung, on which boots and clogs, sides of bacon, oatcakes and any groceries which need to be kept dry are packed. More articles hang from hooks on the beams. The fireplace, lustrous with the polishing of generations, occupies nearly the length of one side, and from its glowing fire comes the fragrant odour of peat. In an arm-chair before it the farmer smokes his clay pipe, and watches the kettle hanging from a steel bar and hook which slides on a crane along the top of the fireplace. The dalespeople call these hooks on which they hang their kettles and huge pans with the handle in the middle, 'reckins,' a shortening of 'reckincruke.' In the will of Dame Ann Lademan, a prioress of Marrick Priory, near Reeth, a 'recking croke' is mentioned along with 'a spete, cobyerones, a rosting yeron, a brasse potte and a fyer chawfe.' Many of the fireplaces have three or four 'reckins,' all shining brilliantly. They add to the cheerfulness of these farm kitchens, which are the living-rooms of the family, and a great part of whose charm lies in the fact that everything in them is for use.

The path from Dalehead crosses a bridge, and goes along flat meadows by the river. At Hoggarth's Bridge the road is reached again. It is evening, and looking back you see the sun like a burnished shield. The knight who holds it is the fell creeping down to protect the valley. Even after it has vanished the radiance of that shield stays in the sky; and the reflection of it bathes the valley in a rosy glow.

Raven Seat

CHAPTER IV

THE HAMLET OF RAVEN SEAT

You start out for Raven Seat along the same Kirkby Stephen road, but on this shorter journey there is more time to linger. A muffled roar in the distance grows louder as two waterfalls appear—Rainby Falls on the Swale, and Currack Falls on the West Stonesdale Beck. Coming near to each other from different ways, they seem to have tried which could be the lovelier. Beyond them the road turns up to Tan Hill over a bridge crossing the Swale.

This corner is known as Bridge End. A cottage stands there, the door of which opens cheerily on to the road across a patch of cobble-stones. A narrow flower-bed runs round the house, and roses climb up it in summer—a luxury in these parts. In the mining days this house was four 'livings.'[1] Now only a shoemaker and his mother occupy it. The son makes and mends boots and clogs in a low room at the back. Clogs are still the chief footwear in Swaledale, for nothing stands the wet so well. The people get accustomed to their heaviness, and like their roominess. Shoes are for better

---

[1] 'Living' is a local word for a dwelling.

wear; a child coming to school in them would be an exception.

The garden of the shoemaker's cottage runs down to the flat, worn rocks which edge the river here. Mother and son will show with pride the mark on the shop door to which the water rose in the disastrous flood of 1899. Sometimes they wish the fells did not rise so closely in front of the cottage, shutting off the view. But they have only to step out of the door to see the wooded valley running down to Keld with one hillock poking above the rest, as if it had peeped up to see what was happening, and a gay little tree waving its branches proudly on the summit.

A field's length higher up, the hill on the other side of the river rises into the rocky cliff of Cotterby Scar. Under the shadow of this cliff, where the road comes close to the river, are Wainwath Falls with a deep pool at their foot. The border of grass between the river and the cliff seems to be a rabbits' meeting ground; there is generally a black one amongst them. It is also a haunt of dippers and sandpipers, who love to explore the banks. A ruined smelt-mill across the road stands aloof and deserted.

In August the pool below Wainwath Falls is a favourite bathing-place for the scouts who are allowed by Lord Rochedale to camp every year in the shooting-lodge at Keld. The men and boys of the village turn out on Sunday to see the scoutmaster and one or two bigger boys climb up the cliff, walk gingerly along the slippery edge of the fall, poise for a moment over the rushing water, and then leap out beyond it. It makes a diving-board which the gods themselves might have chosen. A dalesman, asked if he ever came to swim in the pool, said: 'Nay, I reckon we git ower-much watter i' these parts to git weeat when we aren't bund.' The falls seem gentle enough when the boys bathe there, but heavy rain can change their aspect in a few hours, for the volume of water which widens the falls also shortens them by filling up the pool.

The lane to Raven Seat and Whitsundale goes through a gate on to another bridge and up the hill-side, passing the farm-house of Smithy Holme, beyond which it dwindles into a boggy path across the fell. The beck runs on the left through a canyon, known as Red Gulch Gill. Then the hamlet appears in the distance, nestling beside the stream, with the fells behind it breaking out here in patches of pink soil instead of peat. It is an hour's walk from Keld.

Raven Seat now consists of two farm-houses, but eleven families once lived there, most of the men being employed in a coal-pit at Tan Hill. Though its population has dwindled there is no air of ruin, rather an atmosphere of well-being. Its buildings rest cosily on the meadows. You drop down to it from all points of the moor as to a haven. A closer knowledge will reveal how like the place are its people in the kindly welcome they give.

The surplus cottages have long been turned into barns, and the same fate has befallen the little chapel, which is now only distinguishable from other barns by one or two tiny, pointed windows. The existence of a chapel in so remote a spot is interesting. It is thought to have belonged to the Inghamite sect, and to have served the outlying farms also, but it had no resident minister. Until five or six years ago, when it was pulled down and destroyed, the pulpit stood in one corner.

Two old men in Raven Seat told us of hard winters in the dale when the snow covered the windows, and they had to dig themselves out. 'We doa't hev winters like them noo,' they said. But for five days in the winter of 1933 the upper dale was completely cut off; no food or mails reached it. In Keld some of the drifts stretched from the cottage roofs across the road, and the men had to dig a way, first from their houses and then along the road, until they met another batch of men doing the same. They cut a narrow way through, and gradually widened it. Later, the melting snow ran down the cutting like a river. The two men told also of bad hay-times when most of the hay rotted in the fields, and some of the grass was never cut; and of war-time when the Government compelled them to grow corn, and it had not ripened in November.

It is interesting to watch the sheep-dipping in the new bath at Raven Seat. One farmer generally helps the other. The huddled group of sheep trembles at the brink, each one struggling a little when its turn comes, and then giving in in helpless resignation. They look astonished when pushed out safe, if wet and sticky; and in a few minutes they are placidly cropping the grass in the meadow beyond.

A track over the moor on the north-east side of the hamlet led to Tan Hill. It is now only seen as a darker green line, though it is occasionally used as a cart way from the Westmorland side. When the last family removed from Raven Seat their furniture was carried along it in sledges. It passes Robert's Seat House, a ruined hut in which a gamekeeper lived just before and during the shooting season, in the days when poaching was common. If the poachers got desperate they would attack the gamekeeper. One gamekeeper was shot below the knee on the moors near Robert's Seat House, and told that if he moved he would be shot higher up—a terrifying experience in that lonely place.

A small beck runs straight through Raven Seat into a deserted valley whose overhanging cliffs end in two long waterfalls. Whitsundale Beck curls off to the left. Two fine sycamores below the chapel seem to point the way to a stone bridge over it. From here a path runs up to the farms of Black How, Harker's House, and Hill Top House, and out on to the Kirkby Stephen road. Birkdale Tarn, stretching half a mile across the moor to the west of these houses, is a familiar landmark from the hills. It was dammed at one time to collect water for working the mines at Lonin End. Now the waves lap drearily at its edges, and a feeling of danger surrounds it. Sheep are often drowned in its waters. Seagulls haunt it in great numbers, and breed there in the spring, their unfamiliar cries added to those of the moor birds. Along the shores of the tarn a fine silver sand is found which the people gather and lay on a piece of wood spread with tar for sharpening their scythes in hay-time. There is also good peat near it.

Raven Seat is an excellent place from which to climb Nine Standards Rigg. The path starts up Low Whitsundale Edge on the far side of the hamlet, keeping to the lower slopes, and crosses Whitsundale Beck near some walls. There is no path across the beck, but the way lies up the moor, veering a little to the right.

The nine pillars which give their name to the hill are misleading. Having seen them from various points, the Mallerstang road and the road from Tan Hill to Kirkby Stephen, you expect them to rise as a guide to the summit, but instead they seem to hide themselves. From the top of the Rigg you can see miles of moor, and hardly dare to peer into the distance lest they should be seen leering from another hill. The land dips quickly at the north end to a lower ridge, and on this the nine stones stand.

If the nine standards are illusive they are astounding when they do appear. They stand in an uneven row, built firmly—not in the haphazard manner of a currack—of small stones, and are of various shapes and sizes, some a high dome, others on huge square bases with a pillar narrowing towards the top. Nobody seems to know just why they were put there. Some say they were built by prehistoric men, others that they marked an old boundary, others that they were placed to represent soldiers, and frighten the raiding Scots by making them think that an army was marching over the Rigg. But a more prosaic theory is that they were built by shepherds as a landmark, and to occupy the long hours they had to spend on the ridge when there were several sheep-folds there; the ruins of these sheep-folds still remain.

On the lonely summit, leaning against one of the pillars, we found a shepherd resting for a moment after rounding up and counting one man's sheep before he went on to another's. It is the custom with many of the dale farmers to employ a shepherd among a few of them. This man did the shepherding for nine farmers in the Barras and Stainmore district of Westmorland. His work was to keep the flocks separate, count them, and drive them back to the tops; for sheep, thinking of their own comfort, invariably drift down the fell. The shepherd is not employed all the year round. When the hay and dippings and sales are over, the farmers have time to look after their sheep themselves, and they dismiss the shepherd. However, if they like him and he likes them, he stays in the district, and they give him any odd jobs on the farms during the winter, and he manages to live until they take him on as a shepherd again in May.

The view from Nine Standards Rigg has again that striking contrast of the green Eden valley and the bleak fells behind. As we stood on the ridge we could hear distant thunder and see the clouds rolling over from the Lake District mountains. Lizards darted from under our feet with their queer creaking noise as we made our way down. With the heavy clouds behind, Raven Seat seemed more than ever a haven.

The road back to Keld from Raven Seat is best in the evening, when the hills behind are wrapped in an unearthly mystery, and the hills in front, mellowed and rounded, give a sense of welcome. At Bridge End the untamed dale ends. Here one thinks not only of its fells and rocks and ravines, but of its people. Here there is a shoemaker, and here civilization begins.

Evening, West Stonesdale

CHAPTER V

TAN HILL AND WEST STONESDALE

MANY inns have claimed to be the highest in England—the 'Cat and Fiddle' in Derbyshire, the 'Isle of Skye' in Yorkshire, the 'Kirkstone' in the Lake District. But figures are figures, and, consulting them, one must allow the claim to Tan Hill Inn in Swaledale, 1,732 ft. above sea-level.

The quickest way to reach the inn, four and a half miles from Keld, is up the road which turns to the right at Bridge End. But there are other, more adventurous ways. Most of them start down the lane which slips out of a corner of the square at Keld, as if it could wait no longer to run and explore the valley; a muddy, careless lane, its tumbling walls covered with moss and lichen. A day in Keld does not seem complete if you have not wandered, if only for a few minutes, down it. It is unthinkable that there was ever a time when it did not start travellers out gaily in the morning, and bring them back contentedly at night.

There is a barn in a field on the top side of the lane with the letters IADARA and the date 1687 carved in relief above the whitewashed window. This was built from the stone of a ruined cottage in Keld over whose doorway the inscription stood. The letters are probably the initials of the people who built the house, who may have been three brothers called Alderson, a name still common in the dale. It was a practice in the seventeenth and eighteenth centuries to carve initials over doorways, and there are many examples in Swaledale.

Presently the lane forks, and the lower path drops down to the bridge. Across the valley are the East Gill Falls, the final spurt of the East Gill Beck before it empties itself into the Swale. This is a tempting beck to explore, wooded at first, but treeless as it nears the moor. A gate opens on to a narrow wooden bridge across the Swale. Before the fateful flood of 1899 there was an old stone pack-horse bridge here. That, alas! is lost, but the beauty of the river remains; through its shallow water you can see the stones at the bottom, and trout darting up for flies. Looking upwards, the village chimneys rise above the cliff; downwards, the banks slope up to the rocky side of Birk Scar.

The path climbs steeply to the left past East Stonesdale farm, one of the best farms in the district. The farm-house nestles into the hill-side, its door opening on to smooth stones, beyond which is a walled garden where gooseberries grow if they do not flourish. Standing there by itself this garden seems an afterthought. A path through a gate to the left and across the fields leads to the ground where the sports are held and out on to the West Stonesdale road. This is the only cart track to the farm, and, but for the fact that there is often a bull in the field, makes a pleasant short walk through Bridge End back to Keld.

The lane between walls leads on to the moor, past the

farm of Frith, standing gaunt on the fell-side, and High
Frith, just beyond it, as cosy as the other is grim. On these
farms the people wrest a living from the high fells, cul-
tivating the few pastures so that they can make hay and
graze their cows, while the moor creeps all round them,
ever on the alert to clutch them back again. You can cross
a tiny beck below Frith's, climb the opposite hill-side to the
road, and turn back to Keld through West Stonesdale. But
for Tan Hill the faint cart track along the fell must be
followed till it meets the road much farther on at a stone
bridge which we shall see again.

An interesting way to reach Tan Hill is over Water Crag,
taking the same walled lane from East Stonesdale, but
turning to the right at the top and making for a gate on the
horizon. From here a 'trod' or 'trodden' drops down to the
beck, and winds up the other side near a shooting-hut. As
you ascend, Great Shunnor Fell and Whernside and the
far-off crest of Ingleborough appear. Their shapes seem to
change as you rise; then they gradually disappear, hidden by
the hill of Rogan's Seat.

The second, not the first currack, marks the summit of
Water Crag, 2,176 ft. The view from here has none of the
startling contrast of the Eden valley seen from High Seat
or Nine Standards, but the immense stretch of unrelieved
moorland is impressive. To the east is the dip which marks
the beginning of Arkengarthdale, and the fells behind it;
to the north the moor, cut by peat crevasses, rolls beyond
Stainmore to Teesdale; and to the west, standing up boldly,
are the pillars on Nine Standards Rigg. At the west end of
Water Crag there are some huge rocks, on the largest of
which a basin is hollowed out, formed by the working of
quartz pebbles against the rock in storms.

It is well to stand occasionally on the way down to Tan
Hill and plan your direction, or peat crevasses too deep to

cross will bar the way; there is no path, but the direction is past a deserted coal-mine, William Gill Pit, and over the moor for a mile. Tan Hill is another illusive landmark. From High Seat and the slopes of Shunnor Fell, even from the road to Bowes on the other side of the moor, the white-washed building shines out, a bright speck in its dark surroundings. But on the way down from Water Crag there is no sight of it until, just when the moor seems to stretch with no break for miles, it suddenly appears nearly on top of you, with a good motor road running past it.

Tan Hill is not boastful about its unique position. A weather-worn sign proclaims it, but this is not aggressive. 'England's Highest Inn,' it says, with a delightful economy of words. The name comes either from the Celtic *tan*, fire, or the O.E. *tan*, a branch. The road to Swaledale branches here. Here the Celts may have lit their Beltane fires to the worship of Baal and the sun.

The inn was much used at one time by pedlars crossing from Westmorland to Yorkshire, and by farmers fetching coal from the mines which dotted this moor. The farm-house near it is now unoccupied, the miners and the pedlars come seldom, and only one shepherd lives with the family at the inn. But the motorists have taken their place—far too many sometimes. Those who wish to see it in its solitude should avoid it on a fine Sunday. And it is solitary on most days, the only sign of life a goat silhouetted against the white wall of the porch. It is worth while arriving on a dull day to see the contrast of the old kitchen with its scoured stone floor, the fireplace hung with gleaming brasses, and a bright list rug before the fire.

For over thirty years Michael Peacock and his wife have kept the Tan Hill Inn. Most of their children were born there, and all of them tramped to Keld and back to school, though sometimes in winter they had to be boarded in Keld during the week. Keld, four and a half miles, and Barras, six miles, are the nearest villages.

In the mining days when the dale was more thickly populated, hound trials were held at Tan Hill, and attracted crowds. Bruising contests fought with bare fists were also popular. The tale is told of a fight between the champion bruiser of Westmorland and George Kearton of Oxnop Hall, near Muker. It was a hard struggle, but the Swaledale man exhausted his opponent and was declared the winner. After the fight the two men, having washed in the same tub, held a carousal at the inn for a week, drinking day and night, as a sign that they were still good friends. This kind of thing does not seem to have had a bad effect on the health of George Kearton, for he died at Oxnop Hall in 1764 at the age of a hundred and twenty-four.

From the rocks behind the inn is seen the desolate expanse of Stainmore. Sphagnum moss grows plentifully here, and was gathered during the war. We once surprised a baby curlew on this stretch; it scuttled in front of us on long, ungainly legs while its mother called and swooped above in agony.

The road to West Stonesdale and Keld turns at right angles nearly opposite the inn. It always feels heartless to turn down this road leaving the inn alone. Its windows seem to gaze pathetically after you as a child watches his parents depart, leaving him to fight his own battles at school. A mile down the road is the entrance to the Tan Hill coal-mine, the largest and most important of the numerous pits which dot the moor round Tan Hill, others being King's Pit, Kettle Pot, the William Gill, and a small pit on the west slope of Shunnor Fell. Their story, like that of the lead-mines, is one of decline; Tan Hill is the last one to be worked, and only two men are employed there.

It is not known when coal was first found on these moors,

but in 1296 12d. was returned as profit from a mine here, and in the fourteenth century a pit named Tackan Tan was leased for 4 marks a year. Some years since a wooden pick tipped with iron was found in the mine, a relic of the days when iron was used sparingly. The last manager had in his possession an indenture made in 1670 between Philip Lord Wharton and three men to whom he leased the mine. The agreement allowed Lord Wharton to take coal free of charge up to a hundred and fifty loads a year for use at his residence, Wharton Hall, Westmorland. At that time Tan Hill and the smaller mines supplied coal to Swaledale, Wensleydale, Arkengarthdale, and Westmorland, and many men were employed. The coal was carried on pack-horses and donkeys; later, as the roads improved, carts were used. For farmers from the lower valleys the journey took two days; they would load their carts with produce from their farms and sell it on the way. There are men still living who can re-member seeing processions of thirty or more carts when they arrived at their work at six o'clock in the morning. One man kept a drove of donkeys near the mine for distributing the coal. The coming of the railway to Hawes and Kirkby Stephen was the first step in the decline. Now motor lorries will deliver what they call 'station' coal anywhere, and the demand for the 'pit' coal, which is harder and dirtier, grows less every year. But this hard coal is more economical than the 'station' coal, and it burns well with peat.

A track leads past the tumbling buildings to the level. This was started about ninety years ago and runs over a mile into the hill; it has always been hampered by water draining in from earlier workings. It is a friendly pit, and, though this may seem a contradiction, a country thing, part of the life of the dalespeople, many of whom have worked there at some time. Surely no coal-mine ever spoilt its sur-roundings less. Hidden in a hollow, you must be close upon

it to see it, and even then it is possible to pass and not
realize what it is. Already the moor has taken to herself
again the tippings which it once turned out. It has its failings.
Sometimes the roof of the level will slowly sink and shut
the miners in at the far end. There they have to wait till their
absence is discovered, and rescuers draw them up through a
convenient shaft. One man coming with a load to the
entrance saw the roof begin to sag, and, bending low,
dragged himself and the pony through just in time.

On the road below, you startle a group of horses grazing
on the moor. As they race away with tossing heads they
might be wild horses on a prairie. But in July they are to be
seen placidly pulling hay in the meadows. When the farmers
did their own carting and carrying, the horses were worked
all the year round. Now, when so much is delivered to their
doors, they only need the full quantity in hay-time, and for
the rest of the year most of them are turned on to the moor.
They get wild and quarrelsome sometimes; one or two have
had to be killed as the result of a kick from another horse.

Just beyond the cart track to Frith the road crosses a
moorland bridge. Patches of moss creep over its walls,
whose stones have taken unto themselves the colours of the
moor. We have sat by this stream hoping to see a wheatear
go into her nest under the arch. She perched on the bridge
and watched us, sometimes swooping under it to glance at
her babies, then darting away over the moor in fright, to be
back on the bridge again in a few minutes. Wild ducks fre-
quent the beck just above the bridge, making their nests on
the rushes by the banks. Moorland trout are plentiful, as
they are in most of the high becks of Swaledale.

A little past the bridge, edges of peat crevasses line the
road, and trunks of birch-, nut-, and pine-trees can be seen
deeply sunk into the peat. These trees do not now grow as
high as twelve hundred feet above sea-level. A vast forest

covered the moors after the Ice Age, but the ground has since become too peaty and boggy, and the climate too rainy for trees to grow. The trees probably stood the colder conditions for centuries. Relics of the old forest at Keld show what they looked like.

This is a good district for peat. It is cut in June. First the grass and heather are pared off the peat-bed, then the peat is cut out in convenient sizes, and left to dry. In a few days, when they have hardened a little, the pieces are reared against each other and left till they are dry enough to bring away and stack. In a wet season the peat never dries, and cannot be gathered. Not nearly so much peat is cut on the moors to-day. Like the burning of lime for the land, the practice seems to be dying out. There are lime-kilns on most farms, but none are used.

There is nothing to prepare you for the hamlet of West Stonesdale, no gentle working down to meadows, for it is actually on the fells. It has been cited as one of the remotest hamlets in England. There is abandonment in its cottages looking straight on to the open moor, a gipsy element only modified by the neat gardens in front. This freedom has its disadvantages. One woman who removed to a hamlet a few miles down the dale felt stifled with another cottage facing her across the road.

In the middle of the hamlet the road takes a bend and the scene changes. The cottages cluster together, and the gipsy element is gone. The houses are old, one is dated 1674, and have more suggestion of architecture about them than most of the simple dwellings. Passing through it from the moors in the dusk, when lamps are lit in the windows, the sudden change from the fells is striking, and the cottages take on a perhaps exaggerated dignity.

When the coal-pits were flourishing, farmers fetching coal would stop for a cup of tea and a chat in West Stonesdale.

If their friendly carts come seldom now, the monotony is broken in other ways, for motor trials run through it, one of the features being Silver Hill between West Stonesdale and Bridge End. Only since 1932 has a red sign pointed out the dangerous bends on this hill. In the fields near it purple gentians grow in August.

Crackpot Hall

CHAPTER VI

CRACKPOT HALL AND SWINNERGILL

THE farm-house of Crackpot Hall, gazing defiantly across at Kisdon from its lofty site, arouses one's curiosity and imagination the moment it is seen from the village of Keld, from East Gill, or from Muker and the hills beyond. There are more remote houses, but none with quite that untamed air. It is one of the places which the lane from Keld sets out to find. Crossing the wooden bridge the path turns to the right over a smaller bridge above East Gill Falls, and runs, mounting all the time, along the side of Rogan's Seat, 2,203 ft. The lower slopes are meadow-land, and are called Hall Out Pasture, being part of Crackpot Hall farm.

Presently the hill-side below the path is covered with stunted trees, their trunks and branches thickly grown with lichen, elm, hawthorn, mountain ash, yew, silver birch, oak, ash, sloe, and bird cherry with its white, showy blossom. This is all that remains near Keld of the forest which at one time covered the land here. Herds of red deer roamed in this forest, and there was much hunting. Crackpot Hall itself was built as a shooting-lodge for Lord Wharton when he hunted the deer on this part of his estate. Not until 1725 did the red deer vanish from Swaledale; this was much later than in many parts of the country, probably because the estate was owned privately, not by the Crown. One reason for their going was that much of the forest where they lived was destroyed by fumes from the smelt-mills.

From a bend in the road there is a magnificent sight of the gorge through which the Swale flows here, the slopes of the forest dipping down to the rocks and the river. Farther on, the fell above the path is thick with bracken, a curious sight in the spring when the new plants push up their long, leafless stalks, looking as though a plague of caterpillars has swept them, the buds curling over at the top like caterpillars themselves. Bracken is cut and dried for bedding; the distance from Richmond makes the carting of straw far too expensive.

Crackpot Hall has a majestic situation. Far below in the valley the river curves serpent-like, its pebbly bed stretching wide on both sides, and the fells rolling grandly back from the meadows which line its banks. The house standing proudly above it seems to exult in its position. What cares it for wind and storms when it can gaze down on this?

Probably owing to the mine-levels under it, the foundations of Crackpot Hall slipped many years ago, and now the tops of the doors and windows are at all angles, and the bedroom floors tilt like the rolling deck of a ship. Another relic of the mines is that hens cannot live there; it is thought that they pick up some poison from the lead.

The children at Crackpot Hall are untamed like their home. Until they go to school and lose a little of their naturalness they are spirits of the moors, running barefoot among them, clambering like animals over the loose stone walls, which are high and hard to scale on this hill-side. Once as we sat gazing at the distant view of Keld, there was a sudden rush from behind, our caps and sticks were snatched away and hurled over the wall, and a tiny figure clambered after them with a mocking, chuckling laugh—that was Alice at four years old, Alice with the madness of the moors about her, and all their wariness. 'Ah, ye're plaguin' me,' she said, when we offered her a pencil and some paper to draw on, all we had with us. Most of her speech is in so strong a dialect that it might be a foreign tongue. She had been lost and found fast asleep in a gully or a hay-field far from the house. We think of her rolling down the steep meadows with a fat sheep-dog puppy; marching along the rough lane followed by two white cats; yes, and clean and smart at the chapel anniversary or the sports. Her eager face, its keen eyes framed by fair, tumbled hair, is to us a part of the fascination of Crackpot Hall.

Except for one small field on the top of a ridge, there is not any flat land on Crackpot farm, but much of the grass is grown and cut for hay. The hay harvest in this district is often as late as the corn harvest in lower country; this is owing partly to its height, and partly to the fact that the sheep and lambs are grazed in the meadows until the last lambs are a fortnight old and can be turned on to the fells From very early spring hay-time is the chief thought in the minds of the people. The winter's feed for their stock depends upon it; if it is scanty there will be bills for hay and carting, and if it is poor there will be more cattle cake to buy. The farmers are pleased to see the sun because it will bring on the grass; but a few 'shooers' are welcome in between, for the moisture soon drains off the steep fields with little depth of soil above the rock. When hay-time comes, generally towards the middle of July, everything else is put on one side. All the women help, extra daughters appearing miraculously from service. Irishmen are some-times employed by farmers with small families. In a very wet summer much of the hay has to be left to rot in the fields, and some of the grass is never cut. When hay-time is well and safely over, a wave of relief goes through the upper dale.

The dale methods of haymaking are different from those of lowland districts. The hay is raked into windrows, after which a wooden contrivance, something like a snow plough and pulled by a horse, is often used to push it together. If it is not to be led immediately, it is made into large cocks called 'pikes.'

If the hay is far from a barn it is piled on to a wooden sledge for leading. Carts are not used for this, or indeed much other work on the farm. Even where they could go the farmer thinks it a waste of energy to pile up the hay only to pull it down again. Sledges are used for most jobs, large ones for the hay, and low, squat ones, called coup carts, for carting manure and cattle food.

There are no haystacks, unless there has been an unusually good crop with a mild winter preceding it so that not much hay has been used for the sheep, when the farmer might make a very small, round stack in a sheltered corner. As a general rule, all the hay is stored in the barns, of which there is one to every two or three fields. These two-storied barns of grey stone dotting the hill-sides are a familiar sight. They lessen the labour of the farmer in the winter, for the hay is kept in the top stories and saves much heavy carrying to the stock. Cattle are housed in the lower stories.

The path to Swinnergill, passing under the shadow of Beldi Hill, whose sides are scarred with the tippings of what was a very rich mine, goes behind the hall and up to a little gate; then along the slope of the Swinnergill Ravine, under Buzzard Scar. This is a grim, treeless valley. A little way up where it is joined by East Grain Gill there are more extensive remains of lead-mines. We have seen a pied stoat creep stealthily up this hill-side, and add a sinister air to the scene. It is a good walk up East Grain and over the moor to Gunnerside.

Beyond East Grain the Swinnergill Ravine narrows into a gorge, and the way lies up the bed of the stream, until it is suddenly stopped by the Swinnergill Falls. The gorge widens out at the foot of the falls into a kind of room shut in on all sides; and this part is known as Swinnergill Kirk. A cave lies to the left of the falls, the entrance almost hidden by spray. In the seventeenth century, when Nonconformists were fined for holding meetings, zealous Christians would journey to remote places to hold a service. Swinnergill Kirk was one of these meeting-places. A scout would be stationed on the fell above where he could watch all approaches. At the first note of warning the service would be stopped, and the people run into the cave for shelter. The cave is low at the entrance, and you must stoop to enter, but it lifts in a few feet to the height of a room, though it never widens into more than a broad passage. It was also used as a shelter by fugitive Scots after their retreat from Derby, some of whom, fearing to continue the journey back, settled in the dale.

It is generally cold and draughty in Swinnergill Kirk. The wind moans above, and leaves float mournfully into it one by one. A tiny tree leans stiffly over the falls, and a few stunted ones above it slowly nod their heads as if they heard echoes of hymns long silent. Some of the water from the falls turns back into the cave, and forms an undergound stream which comes out again in East Gill. Above the kirk, Swinnergill is a merry moorland stream with miniature waterfalls and clear pools. You can follow it and drop down to Arkengarthdale, or turn to the west to climb Rogan's Seat, 2,203 ft.

A path along Ivelet Side, on the east slope of the ravine, leads to where a narrow bridge crosses the Swale, and from there joins the old Corpse Way to Grinton, to continue along Ivelet Side through Calvert Houses to Gunnerside. But to return to Keld you must cross the bridge on to Muker Carrs, and turn back on to a path through the meadows on the Kisdon side of the river. In stormy weather the Swale rushes through these meadows more like a Canadian river, and hundreds of tiny springs bubble up in the marshy grass. In the spring the cuckoo is seldom silent here, and two small, angry birds can often be seen chasing the great, browny-grey one from the region of their nest.

In the mining days this path was a cart track to Keld. In a ruined cottage to the left, called Hartlakes, a miner once lived who worked at Tan Hill; he used to ride to his work in a donkey cart, and bring it back at night full of coal which he sold on the way. Now the cottage is a ruin, its floors falling in and its garden thick with nettles. Farm workers have sheltered in it while haymaking, and have written on its walls records of the weather and the state of the harvest for many years. Travellers have come back to it, some of them descendants of men and women who lived there, and have written who they are and where they now live. As you approach the house its little windows seem to blink expectantly, as though it hopes that at last someone is coming to live in it again.

Farther on an inconspicuous wooden gate leads down to Kisdon Falls, which can only be reached from this side of the river. It is a scramble down, and there is nothing to point the way, for Swaledale is modest about its beauty spots. But of all the Swale falls this has been the most extolled; Speight and others thought it well worth comparison with any in Western Europe. It comes in two falls over high rocks with a pool between them, where it seems to gather strength for the second effort. Cliffs shut it in on either side, and around it there is complete solitude.

As you return, the noise of the fall grows fainter, and slowly the stillness of the valley descends again, wrapping you as it were in a spell, so that everything but this fairy-like beauty is forgotten. Then the path runs on to a more open space where rocks break through the turf, and grassy mounds are crowned with stunted trees. There is a touch of enchantment here. Surely on moonlight nights fairies dance over the knolls and play hide-and-seek behind the trees; they would never let so perfect a place be wasted!

Thus the dreamy lane wanders back to Keld. Smoke curls lazily up from cottage chimneys, and on the fell across the river the farmstead of East Stonesdale, vague and shadowy, nestles into the hill-side for warmth and comfort from the night.

Angram

CHAPTER VII

KELD TO THWAITE

Once the wrench of leaving Keld is over and the Cat Hole Inn passed, the charm and interest of the haphazard road which wanders down to Thwaite lays hold of you. There is a keen pleasure in following a river up a valley, but is there not a rarer enjoyment in following it down? In going up your eyes and mind are set upon the heights, and the rest is viewed with slight impatience as only on the way. With the achievement and labour over, there is time and inclination to linger and explore, and the beauties of the valley are enhanced by the vivid knowledge of the hills behind.

It is never dull, this road to Thwaite, now capering in a switchback, now curving into the hill-side by a barn or cottage. There are people, some of them dalespeople, who hope and declare that one day a broad highway will run

64

through the bottom of the valley to take the place of this which skips along the hills. One hopes the idea will lead to nothing more than did the talk of a railway up the dale thirty or forty years ago.

The first lane on the left is where the Corpse Way started from Keld over Kisdon. Beyond it on the right another lane turns up to the hamlet of Thorns, composed of a few cottages placed high above the road in the very heart of the hills. Tall sycamores and ash-trees, unbent by wind or weather, are grouped round it. A grindstone, a round stone fixed to a stand, and turned by an iron handle, stands by a farm-gate. Every farm has its grindstone, varying from large, new-looking ones to tiny, worn ones—proof of the sharpening of many sheep shears.

A bend in the road brings you to Aygill—one farm-house and a country cottage made out of two. The gill which runs down to Skeb Skeugh Beck in the valley is in a hollow between two hills, so deep that even on the wildest days there is shelter; a 'loun' spot, the people call it, meaning 'sheltered.' 'Ah mun finnd a loun spot,' a man will say if he wants to light his pipe in a wind.

The farm-houses which follow, two named Greenses, then Crag Hall, are long buildings standing below the level of the road. These houses, whilst possessing their own character, have one point in common: their windows face the road where the hill across cuts off the view, and they present blank walls to the country behind. In the days when the houses were built, the side which faced the weather was left with as few openings as possible; no one thought of the view, it was chance if the cottage looked on to one. Until a few years ago most of the windows in the dale had small square panes whose only means of opening was a hinge on one of the squares; often the bedroom windows had no opening at all. Most of these have been replaced by sash windows, which, though not so picturesque, are certainly healthier. Sash windows are a kind of fetish with the women, who grumble and complain until they get them. But they must be sash windows; casements seem to have no attraction for them.

The road dips down past Crag Hall, and then climbs swiftly up to Angram, where the houses cluster on the top of the hill as if they have been blown up there from both sides. We have lived during long, sunny days, and grey days too, in the farm-house on the low side of the road, which the farmer, having rented the farm belonging to it as well as her own, is willing to let. Apart from this there are now only two houses occupied in Angram.

Imagine standing at one's back door looking up the grassy valley to Keld, with the beck like a streak of quick-silver, and across it the bulk of Kisdon, far enough away not to be overpowering. Picture having breakfast on a rickety round table outside, while the heat lies in a gentle haze over the hill-side, and in the valley a woolly mist rolls and curls, hanging lingeringly over it for a time, then quickly gliding up it as though swept by an invisible brush, leaving the heat in a dancing sheen behind.

Here is a scene of peace and solitude, but the other side of the house has a different aspect. Before it goes the life of the dale, slowing down to pass through its narrow road. All the doors and windows face this way, looking so closely on to the farm-house across that conversation is possible without coming outside. The strains of wireless waft over, for nearly every cottage has a wireless set—perhaps it sooner than anything else will rob the dalespeople of their individuality. Or you hear the swish, swish of the daily swilling of the stone flags and steps and wall-tops, swilling which with the years has worn the stone to the smoothness of china.

Here the mail van, heralding its coming by the roar of the engine up the hill, stops on its way to Keld; and the postman gets out to start his long delivery with a greeting for everyone. The real day seems to begin with his arrival, for the dale farmers, with little stock to milk and feed and few men to attend to, are not early risers. Here the mail van slows down at night, and the driver snatches the letters for posting as he passes.

Past this door go the processions of sheep to the sales and shows. Closely packed together, they move like a dark river down the narrow road, each flock heralding its coming by the clop, clop of its pattering feet. Behind them a farmer rides a sturdy dales pony, a spare yeoman walks with swinging stride, or a yeoman's son with cap on one side and a gay scarf adds a note of colour. A woman stops her work to call out a word of good luck as the flock patters past her door. An old man, too lame and infirm now for long tramps, gives a greeting. It is all very friendly, for everybody knows everybody.

One of the noisiest days is when the roadmen appear to tar the road. Walkers justly complain of the extravagant use of tar on the Swaledale roads, and the hard grey tone of the gravel with which it is covered—the colour of the Mallerstang road is much more attractive. The people of Angram are concerned about the streams of uncovered tar left at the edges close to their steps, but they thoroughly enjoy haggling with the roadmen about it.

We remember a little batch of chickens which suddenly decided to cross the road while the tar was uncovered. They had a dreadful journey. Each step was an agony, and once or twice they almost gave up in despair. Then, in their glee at finally getting across, they flew excitedly on to each other's backs as half-grown chickens do, and the result was disastrous. We suppose they would recover when they moulted, but for weeks their tale of woe was plain to all who passed.

The tall house at the top of the hill is always known as 'Up t' steps,' because a flight of steps leads up to it from the road. In 1830, still the prosperous days of lead-mining, one John Fawcett started to build 'Up t' steps' for an inn, but his money gave out before it was completed, and another man finished it for a house. A narrow room opening on to the top of the steps was evidently intended for a bar; but the more imposing front faces the other way on to Skeugh Head Lane. A few years after it was finished a charity school for girls was held in one of its rooms, started by a lady named Mrs. Cope who used to stay at the shooting-lodge at Keld. The girls were taught reading and writing and how to work samplers. An old lady now living higher up the dale has a sampler which her mother worked at this school. The cross-stitch reads: 'Nanny Fawcett worked this sampler at Mrs. Cope's Charity School at Angram, aged 10 years, 1844.' At much the same time a small school for boys was started in a house, now a barn, lying in a field on the high side of the road between Angram and Crag Hall.

Education seemed to flourish in Angram at the beginning of the nineteenth century, for a cobbler is said to have kept an evening school in another cottage. He held his classes in the kitchen, which had a low, timbered ceiling, and deep cupboards and shelves sunk into the wall on both sides of the fireplace. His pupils had neither books nor slates, but did their exercises and watched the schoolmaster give his lessons with chalk on the smooth flags of the floor. The pupils were all past childhood, and many would tramp miles for their bit of learning. It was before the days of free education, and each would pay a small sum for his lessons. Before education became compulsory the farmers and miners refused to send their children long distances to school.

Angram was then much more thickly populated. There were 'livings' in what are now barns, and all the farm-houses held more than one family. Two ruined cottages were also 'livings,' one retreating shyly at an angle from the road, and the one in which the cobbler taught standing boldly at the top of the hill looking down to Thwaite with a view whose breadth and grandeur never loses its freshness. These two cottages were taken mostly by newly married couples when the husband was still a farm-man on his father's or some other farm. Many farmers in the dale started their married life in one of them. In these days of smaller families, the newly married people often stay at one of their own homes till they get a farm.

Nearly opposite to the cottage with a view, a small, walled-in piece of land attached to a barn is said to have been used as a burial-ground, in the days when funeral processions had to follow the Corpse Way. Those who were too poor or too careless to pay for the journey to Grinton, buried their dead in such small burial-grounds as this at Angram. It seems a happy resting-place, near familiar sights and sounds.

The grazing for the farms at Angram is of tremendous area, stretching six or seven miles on to the moors as far as Great Sleddale. Here, far from other cultivation, there are a few walled meadows where, enclosed from the fells, grass is grown for hay. Walls mark the boundaries of the farms for a little way up the fells; later it is open moor with only an invisible boundary, and the sheep wander as they please. A farmer here does not employ a shepherd, and only goes up to the sheep himself every two or three weeks, unless it is very hot or snowy, to drive back any which have strayed far from his share of the common. He picks out his own sheep by the mark, not by actually counting them, so that from the time he turns them back on to the fells with their lambs until they are brought together to be dipped he does not know just how many he has.

The way which the farmer takes from Angram to Great Sleddale starts as a lane between walls which is part of an old track into Westmorland. There are signs of very early habitation in this hamlet 1,185 ft. above sea-level. Distinct remains of ancient earthworks on the hill-side behind the village, and its name, show that farming was carried on here long before the Conquest.

The name Angram, from the Old English *anger*, of which the dative plural is *angr*, a meadow or clearing, and *ham*, a home, fits in with the meaning of Skeugh Head Lane which comes from the Norse *skogr*, a wood. The lane runs behind the hamlet and leads to two or three farms. Heather, never far from Angram, creeps down to its edges. In a gully near it the boys from one of the farms showed us a ring ouzel's nest, and higher up, in a clump of grass overhanging a pool, a wheatear's. The boys, who are clever at finding the nests, will creep stealthily from one to another to see how they are progressing; then as a reaction from so much quietness they will rush madly down the moor, each seize a worn motor tyre, and race along the road bowling them like hoops.

The women of the dale are busy from morning to night, but they have always time to stop and talk. They welcome any diversion, and go back to work again cheerfully when it is over. We have to thank Angram for giving back to us, at least for a time, the capacity to stand and stare. Set hours for work are unusual. Sacks of coal will arrive at half-past ten at night, and if one is 'abed' there is sure to be someone in the morning with time to 'hug 'em in.'

Winter evenings are occupied with quilting, an art which has died out in many parts of the country. In Swaledale the heavy quilted covers take the place of both blankets and eider-downs. The work is done on wooden quilting frames, and rolled over as it progresses. The quilts are made of two lengths of sateen or cotton with a padding of cotton-wool between them, held together with a running stitch. A favourite method is to join alternate strips or squares of plain and figured material for one side, using all plain material for the other. The patterns are cut out in cardboard, and pencilled or dinted with a needle on to the material. These patterns are handed down from one generation to another; the fern pattern, the star, the Prince of Wales's feathers, the bellows and star—known as 'bellis and star'—the twist, and the plate pattern are among them. Some of the quilts are most attractive, and when they have faded a little have a lovely old-world look. On everyday ones the quilting is simple, but best ones, usually those given to a bride, are of plain material on both sides and very elaborately quilted with almost every pattern introduced.

Another industry among the women is the making of list rugs, the main floor-coverings both downstairs and upstairs. In many houses the making of a list rug is also an occupation for winter evenings. At Angram the starting of one is the beginning of a week of feverish activity to which all the spare time of the women of the family and that of any friends and relations who are willing is devoted. The hamlet seems to hold its breath, and lo! in four or five days there is the finished article. The menfolk do not like the huge frames about, and grumble until the work is done.

The dales men and women may talk, but they do not give themselves away. When it is a matter of business they can be close, and ready with an evasive answer. Among themselves they speak a dialect too broad for strange ears to understand. It is pleasant to listen to, having much of the soft Westmorland burr in it. Dalespeople do not address each other with 'Good morning,' or 'Good afternoon.' They have lived too long in conflict with the weather to say 'Good morning' when it is blowing a hurricane or scorching the grass. They greet each other much more literally than that.

'Stormy, Ambrose!'

'Aye, bad, Tom.'

'Fine day, Sarah.'

'It's heeat!'

'Sleeatin', Bill.'

'Aye, we're in for a storm.'

'Droughty, Sam.'

'Thoo's reet, George. We could deu wi' a drop o' rain to start t' grass.'

'Terble cowd!'

'Aye, Lizzie, like snaw.'

'Shooery weather!'

'Shooery.'

A much more interesting proceeding than our stereotyped greetings. If you persist in a towny 'Good morning,' the dalesman will answer 'Good day,' but with an unaccustomed air.

From Angram you look down to Skeb Skeugh Beck, which has valiantly taken the place of the river in this valley. It flows so swiftly and silently through the meadows after storms that in a wet season many lambs are drowned in its innocent-looking waters. We once pulled a lamb out of it ourselves. The mother, after running backwards and forwards for a time in consternation, had given up hope and wandered away to a sweeter patch of grass. But she was pleased to see it back, and the two ran away together bleating contentedly, though as we climbed the hill to Angram we saw them cropping the grass at the edge of the beck again.

Across Skeb Skeugh Beck the meadows and fells form the lower slopes of Kisdon, on which was the Hewker Mills lead-mine, a small mine said to be the oldest in Swaledale.

An old farmer told us, with pride and a little awe, that there was 'hundtheds o' punds wuth o' leead i' Kisdon yet.'

If this valley is not strictly Swaledale, it has all the character of Swaledale; and Kisdon, instead of dividing, is a link which joins it to the other. Leaving Angram the road drops swiftly down to the hollow where Thwaite lies.

Thwaite in its Hollow

CHAPTER VIII

THWAITE AND SHUNNOR FELL

THE name Thwaite, coming from the Scandinavian *thveit*, a clearing, suggests that the Norsemen cleared a space for their settlement from surrounding forest. The forest has now gone, but there is shelter and quiet in Thwaite for those who find the higher villages too bleak.

Cradled in the hills of Kisdon, Shunnor Fell, and Lovely Seat, its position, which seems safe and secure, has in the past been a dangerous one. In the days when wolves swarmed the country-side they would come down from the hills in the winter and lurk around the farm-houses in the village. And it was disastrously placed for the flood of 1899. The force of water which swept down Stockdale came full upon it, taking sheep, dogs, roofs, and hen-houses before it. Had it lasted a few more minutes there would have been nothing left of Thwaite. At Hoggarth's, to which the water rushed from the other side of Shunnor, there was one farm-house in danger, but here there was a whole village. The cottage gardens near the beck were washed away, and, ironically, the flowers from them now bloom at Muker.

Thwaite has not yet recovered from the tragedy. Coming close on the failure of the lead-mines, it left the village help-less. There were so few people that there seemed no need to build the damaged houses up again, and not even another generation has had the heart to remake the gardens by the beck.

But the village is gradually coming into its own again. It has always had an affectionate place in the hearts of the people. Farmers, perhaps because of the contrast, choose it to retire to from their wind-swept farms. Most of the families in the upper dale have some association with it, a relation who lives or has lived there. They have memories too of Thwaite Fair in the days when it was an important event of the year, the last of the autumn fairs, except St. Luke's Fair at Kirkby Stephen.

There is an old lady who remembers the excitement of walking down to Muker with her sister on the morning of Thwaite Fair to buy her first pair of shoes. Before then she had worn clogs all day, even for chapel and Sunday school. On their way the two girls met a man who was known as 'Grain Dick Anty' his name being Grainger, his father's Dick, and his grandfather's having been Anthony. This habit of ignoring the surname is still common, a person being known as Bob Jim Jack, or Maggie Libbie, or Kirsty John Kit. Grain Dick Anty stopped the girls and asked them: 'Whar's ta gaen?' When they told him their errand he gave them twopence each for a 'fairing.' 'And that,' said the old woman, 'was t' first monny we ivver had for sweets or sike-like i' oor lives.'

Up to the beginning of the twentieth century the sheep

brought down to Thwaite Fair in the middle of October stretched far up the hill to Angram on one side, and to the Hawes road on the other. They were sold privately, not by auction. The day was treated as a holiday. At that time a pack of hounds was kept at Low Row, and this was brought to hunt for hares on Kisdon on the morning of the fair. The hares which they caught were 'bossed' (boiled) along with a sheep at the inn; and a supper was made of the 'bossed' hare, beer, and oatcake. Thwaite only possesses a temperance hotel to-day, but at that time this was an inn called the 'Joiner's Arms.' A dance was held in the front room of the inn on the night of the fair. The beer shop at the back, where the men sang all night, was so popular that there was only standing room. Some of the farmers stayed a week in Thwaite drinking away the money which they had received for their sheep. This habit of drinking for days after some festival, as did the two bruisers at Tan Hill, seems to have been prevalent in the dale. There was a man at Gunnerside who, after he had collected his rents, went into the inn, and did not leave his chair until he had spent all he had collected.

The auctions for sheep at Hawes have taken the trade from local fairs like this at Thwaite. The small number of pens now required are put up in an open space at the roadside, and the business is soon over. But old customs and ideas change slowly, and an air of holiday still persists in Thwaite on Fair Day, and draws the people. There are no women to be seen outside; they are all shut up in the cottages getting dinners and teas ready. Sisters and nieces, mothers and daughters from neighbouring villages have all come to help. The villagers keep open house that day. The dalespeople are naturally hospitable, and this is the kind of tea they give their friends: white and brown bread and butter and tea-cake, jam, Swaledale cheese—which is very like Wensleydale—biscuits, rock buns, plain cake, currant cake, apple tart, curd tart, jam tart, all of them home-made. The people eat a great deal of pastry. So, if the glory of the fair has departed, it remains as a pleasant meeting in the autumn, a time when the people talk over old days.

Havercakes are seldom made in the dale now, but a few generations ago they were the principal cereal food. The women had one day a week for baking them. The mixture, made of coarse oatmeal and water, is rolled out and laid on a backstone, a kind of gridiron, like a frying-pan without edges, the handle of which goes over the top, and has a swivel which turns as it hangs on the reckin. When baked, the round cake is lifted off and put to dry on a 'cake stool,' a wooden stand like a small easel, with two pegs on which to rest the cake. We have seen one of these cake stools, over a hundred years old, still in use. The cakes were often stored on a rack on the ceiling, called a 'fleeak,' to keep crisp. Anyone coming in could break off a piece and eat it.

On ordinary days a drowsy lethargy hangs over Thwaite, but it wakes to life as the children come tramping home from school, and as the shepherd comes down from the moor, and the farmer appears from his walling or hay-making or fetching down loads of dried bracken or rushes from the fells. Rushes are used for bedding as well as bracken, and for thatching hay and bracken stacks. Soon the children are playing among the stones, or fishing for tiny trout with jam jars in the bed of the beck. A woman will come out to rinse a muddy coat in the water, or scold a child for getting wet. The beck is the centre of the village life.

The two famous naturalists, Richard and Cherry Kearton, were born at Thwaite. It was in exploring its gullies and the moors above them that they developed the love and interest in nature which was to make them famous. A gentleman who came shooting in the dale took an interest in the boys, and helped them on. Their mother was left a widow, and moved away while they were still young, but they never lost their love for Swaledale. Many of the people in the dale are related to them. Their cousin, George Kearton, still lives in the village. As a boy he went to school at Muker with them, and says they soon 'knew mare na t' schulemester.'

In a more majestic manner than the friendly hill of Kisdon, Great Shunnor Fell, rising 2,340 ft. above sea-level, the highest hill in Swaledale, and the fourth highest in York-shire, dominates not only Thwaite but much of the upper dale. From miles up the dale it is seen rising above the rest, and from miles below it can be picked out, still looming high. Part of that great ridge which shuts Swaledale in on the west, it rears its huge bulk between it and Wensleydale, belonging to one as much as the other. Everything about it is on the grand scale. The Buttertubs Pass, one of the highest and widest mountain passes in England, runs over its lower slopes. The name Shunnor comes from the Norse *sjon* and *sjonar*, and means a look-out hill. Eagles at one time nested on its rocks, which is probably the reason for the name Erne being given to one of its buttresses. Clouds often hang round its summit when the other hills are clear. Mists can roll over aggravatingly as you reach the top while the valley below is still bright in the sunshine.

Shunnor Fell can be climbed from Great Sleddale, but a good starting-point is from the moors immediately behind Angram. There is no definite track, though an occasional currack marks the way; often the footprints of shepherds can be followed across the peat morasses. You come upon long, dry stretches, covered with white stones and silvery sand, which look like the dried-up beds of mountain tarns, but which are probably peat beds from which the peat has eroded, leaving exposed glacial drift. During the Ice Age the glacier from Mallerstang joined the one on Shunnor

Fell, their main movement being over Water Crag into Teesdale.

Turning as you ascend, Tan Hill Inn, a white speck which seems to catch every wandering gleam of sun, can be picked out on the hills opposite; a silver streak to the west of it is Birkdale Tarn. The currack below the summit is the best place from which to get an impression of Swaledale, its line of meadows clearly cut against the fells, with Muker resting composedly in the midst, the smoke from its cottage chimneys hanging over it like a caress.

A shepherd once said: 'You can see all t' world from t' top o' Shunnor,' and having stood on its summit, you can understand his feelings. It is in the midst of the Pennines. To the south-east is the hill of Lovely Seat, the ridge of which, sloping down to Muker, is seen from higher up the dale. The name of Lovely Seat is a corruption; it was once Luina Seat or Lunasit, which may have come from the Scandinavian *luin*, a sound or alarum; if so it is an indication that warnings were signalled from it to the Norse settlers in Thwaite. On the Wensleydale side Lovely Seat merges into Stags' Fell, so called because stags once roamed there. Across Wensleydale are Widdale Fell and Dodd Fell, with Cam Fell and Penyghent beyond them, and beyond again the solid summits of Whernside and Ingleborough. Morecambe Bay can be seen through a gap. To the north, Wild Boar Fell across Mallerstang, and the Lake mountains in the far distance, lead round to Mickle Fell and Stainmore. This is a scene of grandeur, but the most absorbing view from Shunnor Fell is that of the two dales of the Ure and the Swale: Wensleydale, broad and fertile, lying low down the fells, its flat pastures like park land; and narrow Swaledale with scarcely one level field, so near the fells that it seems a miracle it ever became a cultivated valley.

Shunnor Fell can be descended down Hearne Beck to

Hardraw in Wensleydale, by following the fence westward down Hell Gill into Mallerstang, or eastwards to the top of the Buttertubs Pass, or by the route down Stockdale to Thwaite. The last route passes a disused coal-mine, and comes into a lane on the north of Stockdale. A farm here known as Moor Close must have been a terrifying place when the cloud burst on Shunnor Fell, for the full force of the water rushed down Stockdale Beck. The lane, seared and cut by storms, comes out into the main road a little above Thwaite.

After leaving the village the Buttertubs Pass turns off to the right. This highway connecting Swaledale with Wensleydale is very old. It was a path in pre-Conquest days, and was made into a cart track when wheeled traffic was first used. Until a few years ago its surface was very rough, and it had an element of adventure for the motorist. Now it is a tarred road. It rises to a height of 1,682 ft. Across Cliff Gill where Lovely Seat merges into Muker Common, the stone walls run up the hills in lines and squares like an old geometrical design whose meaning has long been lost. Near the top are the Buttertubs, deep, rocky holes whose limestone sides have been formed by the action of water. They vary in depth, one being nearly a hundred feet. An old man once declared that some of the Buttertubs had no bottom, and some were deeper than that. In a few the noise of trickling water can be heard, but in most one looks into silent depths. At one time these swallow holes were a danger to travellers in the dark or fog, but most of them are now railed off from the road. Sheep occasionally fall down them, and farmers have to be lowered by ropes to rescue them. Once past the Buttertubs the hills of Wensleydale appear, then, as the road winds down to Hawes, its wider, softer valley. Hawes, though not in Swaledale, is the chief town for the upper dale. To it those flocks of sheep wind over the pass to the sales.

The most important sales are in October, when the pedigree stock from which the farmer draws the greater part of his income is sold. On these days the town seems to overflow. Cars and carts line the narrow streets, and the people fill in the gaps. From early morning and during much of the day before, the flocks of sheep have been arriving.

There is a serious bustle in the sheds where they are to be sold, and in bad years like that of 1932 an anxiety about prices, which each man carries off according to his temperament. It is dark inside and closely packed, the men wedged tightly against the ring through which the sheep are passed and speedily disposed of, a seemingly unending procession. The auctioneer's voice goes on monotonously and indifferently. But there is a friendly feeling, for buyers and sellers know each other well. The sheep are brought in in lots, of from two to about ten. If the bids are not high enough the owner shakes his head and drives them out again, with the prospect before him of trailing them back many miles, and bringing them to try their luck at another sale, if he cannot dispose of them privately. A look of expectancy and a drawing in of the crowd tells that some known stock is coming; even in bad times a really good breeder has no difficulty in finding a customer. Here in the low, fuggy shed with its suffocating smell of sheep is the accumulation of the year's work of the dalesmen; and in the marketing of it there is a simplicity and directness which has long disappeared from our cities. The old way of counting sheep has died out. From one to twenty it was: yan, tean, tether, mether, pip, sezar, azar, catrah, horna, dick, yan-a-dick, tean-a-dick, tether-a-dick, mether-a-dick, bumfit, yan-a-bum, tean-a-bum, tether-a-bum, mether-a-bum, jiggit.

The women do not often come near the sale shed, but they love to visit Hawes on the sale days. The younger ones ride pillion behind their husbands' motor cycles, for no

buses run over the Buttertubs Pass. Others beg a lift to
Hawes in a lorry, and most of them contrive to get there
somehow. We took two friends in the back of the car. The
road was up near Hawes, and as we passed the roadmen
called out: 'T' owd lasses is coming, t' owd lasses is coming,'
at which our two passengers threw up their hands and
shrieked with laughter. 'T' owd lasses' seem to be a custom.
In the busy streets they meet each other between buying the
kettles and pans and lengths of cloth for which they have
been saving. But the men and women wend home again,
and when they have gone Hawes is Wensleydale, not
Swaledale.

Passing the Buttertubs Pass the Swaledale road from
Thwaite goes down to Muker. At one point the beck from
Cliff Gill comes close to the road, pouring over the limestone edge as the Scar House Foss. Past prosperous-looking
farms, and running beside the beck, from which inviting
paths turn over tiny bridges, the road winds into Muker.

Muker Tup Sale

CHAPTER IX

MUKER

To those sketchy travellers who turn into Swaledale from the Buttertubs Pass, Muker is the first village in Swaledale. It is understandable that having reached it they look for nothing better. There is a feeling of security about it, placed as it is so well under the shelter of the fell. Raised above the beck, not clustering round it as Thwaite does, it holds itself aloof, as though it felt it rather beneath its dignity to bother with this little stream when the real river is so near. For the Swale appears again at Muker, and the beck joins it just below the bridge. There is another difference, something we have not met before in the dale communities, for, perched unassumingly on the hill-side, is the first church in Swaledale.

Muker church was built in 1580 as a chapel of ease to Grinton, one of the few churches to be erected in this country during the reign of Elizabeth. Its building, and the consecration of the burial-ground joining it, brought to an end those weary funeral journeys down the Corpse Way to the mother church. Even to-day the cottages reach up to it as though welcoming the church for which they had long waited; and it nestles amongst them with the confidence which comes from the knowledge of being wanted and appreciated. It is a simple building, but it achieves beauty and charm from being in perfect keeping with its surroundings. The rough tower and walls are of the essence of Swaledale.

The aisleless interior has no chancel arch, and one corner partitioned by a low panelling forms a vestry. This was at one time a raised platform on which the musicians sat, using a harmonium, a bass fiddle, several violins, and a clarinet. Then the church had a three-decker pulpit, box pews, and a gallery entered by an outside stone staircase. A few brass tablets decorate the walls, but the church has few claims to antiquity, and these not certainties. The bells are thought to have been brought from Ellerton Priory after the Dissolution. This is very likely, as the priory was attached to Grinton church. Their long narrow shape proclaims them to be later than the fourteenth century. Two stones on the east exterior wall of the chancel are carved with the arms of Coverham Abbey and I H S. It seems probable that these were brought from the Abbey. The church also possesses a silver communion cup made by a York craftsman in 1583. On the wall on either side of the altar the Ten Commandments, in large print, make a constant reminder of their duty to the simple congregation. The church was restored in 1890.

Muker church is at its best arrayed in its Easter decorations. With the innate sense of the fitness of things which the people have if left to themselves, they decorate the interior with flowers from the country-side. The ridges and window-sills, round the pulpit, and any other spaces are filled with moss set thickly with bunches of primroses, and here and there are wood anemones and daisies, with daffodils and flowering currants rising above them. Here, as at Keld chapel, the windows are clear, and through them you see the fells stretch down on either side.

The churchyard for which the people waited so long is a kind of mirror of the upper dale. The names on its graves and memorials, Alderson, Harker, Coates, Clarkson, Fawcett, Rukin, congregated here at the last from their far-off farms and hamlets, are still familiar. Seeing them brings to mind their descendants in the dale to-day. It is curious how little these names have changed, how few have disappeared, and how few fresh ones have taken their places. The people, knowing little of the outside world, have been content to stay where they were born and brought up. New-comers are not welcomed in the dale. After nearly a lifetime spent there an outsider is still a 'foreigner' or an 'incomer.' This is a contradictory quality in a people exceptionally genial and hospitable to visitors.

We like the straightforward wording on one of the gravestones, simply: 'John Alderson. Yeoman.' Others have quaint inscriptions; a stone more weathered than the rest, leaning against the east wall, has this verse, written by a late rector to a Mr. Mseon:

> Near Keld's cold stream, I drew my infantbreath,
> There toiled through life; there closed my eyes in death;
> Reader, seek not my frailties to disclose,
> But learn this lesson at my dread repose;.
> Be just, be good, with caution meet thy doom,
> There's no repentance in the life to come.

As a contrast is this peculiar epitaph, erected over the grave of Edward and Anne Broderick of Summerlodge and Spring End, of which family we shall tell more:

> I want the world to know
> That I know;
> That there is no fame;
> That all life is co-equal;

That deficiency in intellect is the why
Of deficiency in action.
That everything is right;
That every atom vibrates
At its proper time, according to the true results,
Of the forces that went before.

BY THE SON LUTHER.

A communal coffin, in which the corpse was carried to the churchyard and then lifted out, was used at Muker until 1735, when the vicar refused to bury anyone without a coffin.

This old church at Muker has associations for many of the people of the dale, and for those few who have gone out into the bigger world. We once met a girl in London whose grandmother rode to her wedding at Muker church on a white horse, on which she and the bridegroom rode back together after the ceremony, a custom in the dale in those days. Soon after it was built the church took its part against witchcraft. A Quarter Sessions record, dated 1606, reads: 'Ralph Milner of Rashe, yoman, being accused of sorcerie, witchcraft, inchantment, and telling of fortunes, shall make his submission at Mewkarr Church upon Sonday next, in the tyme of Divine Service, and confesse that he hath heighlie offended God and deluded men, and is heartily sorie, and will offend no more.'

The lane which leads to the church climbs past it. Twisty ways turn from it, and shops appear in the most unexpected corners; for Muker is much bigger than appears on just passing through it. The lane runs off at length into the track which follows the Swale below Kisdon to Keld, meeting the Corpse Way as it turns to the bridge and Ivelet Moor. It is from the marshy land near the river here that Muker gets its name, meaning a small, cultivated field. Its variations are interesting. Starting in 1274 as Meuhaker, in 1577 it was Muaker, later Mewacre, and in 1606 Mewker, before it became the Muker of to-day.

Evidence of very early occupation has been found on Muker Common. Mr. Edward Fawcett, of Muker, has numbers of flints which he has picked up there. Several years ago at West Arngill on Ivelet Side a skeleton was discovered buried in a sitting position with arms folded across the breast, and with a large stone laid on the top.

The lane past the church leads also to the field where Muker Show, one of the autumn events in the dale, is held in September; a sloping field, cradled in the fells on which the bracken is at this time already touched with gold. The ring is on the one flat piece at the bottom. Here the cattle and the dales ponies are judged. The riders find their horses useful at the show to get a good view of other events. But the ring at Muker is easy to see, for the ground slopes up from it, making a natural grand-stand. Round it gather the dalespeople, representatives of those names in the churchyard. The sheep-dogs sit patiently under the wall at the far end waiting their turn. And at the top of the field the judging of sheep goes on. Keen eyes sum them up, and the interest never flags, for the price which the sheep will fetch later at the sheep sales depends largely on their winnings at the local shows.

For variety there are the classes in the tents: classes for vegetables and flowers, and children's classes for writing and wild flowers—in a district so prolific in wild flowers this class makes a wonderful show. In another there are the bread and cheese, cakes, butter, ham and eggs, and oatcakes, or 'havercakes,' to be baked on a backstone. One young woman who had won a prize with a lovely, fluffy sponge cake, cut it up and offered a piece to all her friends. This seemed to whet their appetites, and they sampled all the sponge cakes, advising one another to taste a bit of Mary's or a corner of Annie's. Then they came to the oatcakes, and each one nipped off a small piece as she passed.

The steward got desperate as he saw the rounds disappearing. 'Oatcake not to be touched,' he called out, but they took no notice. One woman dodged past him. 'Aye, but I'm having a piece,' she said, 'and I like it best wi' a bit o' butter,' and away she went with a corner of oatcake for a dab of first-prize butter. What could the steward do but shrug his shoulders, and hope that some of the exhibits would last out the show?

An emptiness in the field is a reminder of lunch, held in the village hall, below the church. Here again the catering is local, and the farmers' wives and daughters do the serving; and here again the people have come determined to get their money's worth. They start straight on to plates heaped with beef and salad, passing to pies, trifles, and jellies, with cakes and pastries to fill in odd corners. And then, nicely filled, they are ready for speeches from Lord Rochdale, the president, and other members of the committee; speeches given slowly with a convenient stop after each joke to allow the dalesmen time to digest it. At the end of the lunch a cup[1] is presented to the owner of the best sheep in the show—a great honour, for the standard is high. Then back to the field and the judging again.

It is all over suddenly, for there are no side-shows or amusements to keep things hanging on when the real business is finished; though it has been decided that in future something more will have to be done to attract the people. We are glad to have seen it before that became necessary.

An annual fair, now a concert, held in Muker on the Wednesday nearest to New Year's Day, was called 'Muker Old Roy,' probably because the miners kept up the custom of having a good spree, or 'roy,' as it was called locally, after each fair, as in Thwaite.

[1] This silver cup, given by Lord Rochdale, is competed for each year alternately at Muker, Kirkby Stephen, and Middleton-in-Teesdale, by members of the Swaledale Sheep Breeders' Association.

KELD

KISDON FALLS

The Grassy Valley stretching up to Keld

A Sale at Thwaite

CROW TREES NEAR MUKER

Courtesy A. B. Bull

IVELET BRIDGE

THE OLD GANG SMELTING MILLS

GUNNERSIDE FROM THE ROAD TO CRACKPOT

WINTER, BARGATE GREEN, RICHMOND

An annual tup show and sale is also held at Muker in the field below the vicarage in October. One soon falls into the habit of calling a ram a tup in Swaledale. The tup sales come on when most of the sheep sales are over. A few weeks before, a committee of two or three men go round to the farms and pick out the tups which they think are up to a certain standard. These are marked on the horns, a process known as 'crowning'; and only 'crowned' tups may be brought to the show.

The show starts about nine o'clock, and when the judging is over the sale begins. Being the more important beasts, most of the tups are sold singly. In prosperous times a good tup will fetch about eighty pounds, In the bad year of 1932 the highest bid was twenty pounds, and a first-prize winner mounted no higher than nine pounds ten shillings. For many the bidding did not rise above a pound, a low price when the owner is 'hard up for brass,' as one old farmer declared. 'Nay, ah'se nut selled thee yet,' another remarked as he drove his tup out of the ring. It was a wet day, bitingly cold, and by eleven o'clock the field was a quagmire. But the sun broke through occasionally to reveal snow on Great Shunnor Fell, creeping down to the heather and bracken.

So the village of Muker has its importance in these sheep-farming days, just as in the days of the lead-mines it was a busy mining centre. Nanny Peacock, the proprietress of 'The Farmer's Arms,' who died in the winter of 1933, was fond of talking of those old days. In her childhood she went to the day school at Muker, where the vicar, besides looking after his own and a smaller church, was the schoolmaster; according to Nanny, 'a better yan ner schule-teeachers i' these days.' School began at half-past eight each morning, and ended at five, and there were no Saturday holidays. The girls arrived half an hour before the boys to sweep and dust the room. The old woman would reach over to the window-sill where a plant stood on a pile of books, and bring out from them a Bible in which her brother, at the age of eleven, had written his name in copperplate writing. 'They can't write like that nowadays,' she said; 'they teeach 'em nowt i' these days.' There has been a school at Muker from 1678, when Anthony Metcalfe left fourteen acres of land, producing about twenty pounds a year, in his will, to endow a school.

Nestling under Kisdon, Muker looks across to the hill known as Muker Common, whose lines of walls are seen from the Buttertubs Pass. It is hard to imagine Swaledale without its walls; striking over the fells they, and the grey barns which match them, add a human interest to what might otherwise be bare hills. In some parts they are low and tumbling, in others tall and straight with ridges jutting from them to break the wind. You wonder about the men who made them, and the boundaries which they fixed. They are not so old as is often imagined, for, even after the forests disappeared at the end of the seventeenth and the beginning of the eighteenth centuries, the common land was unenclosed, only the pastures close to the villages being walled. There is an award at Keld which shows that many of the enclosures on Kisdon and Angram Common were made in 1829. Muker Common was enclosed a little earlier. The early seventeenth century enclosures are immediately round the villages. Their older walls can generally be told by the way they follow the lie of the land; later enclosures were planned on paper, not on the actual ground, and in these the lines of the walls are straight.

It is said that the art of dry walling is dying out. Certainly there is now only one professional waller in the Keld district, but he is very proud of his job. The old walls are three or four feet wide at the base, but to-day they are not made more than two and a half feet, narrowing to about a foot at the top. To keep his line and thickness the waller uses a wooden frame like an easel without the back leg. This he fixes into the ground a little distance from the wall on to which he is building, keeping it straight with a plumb-line. Strings are carried from the frame to the sides and top of the wall. Choosing stones which fit on to each other, he works from both sides, and fills in the cavity with rubble. About twice in the height of a wall he places large stones which he calls 'troos' (throughs) to strengthen it. The stones meet in one layer at the top, and on this he puts a row endways for a finish. A good waller will build seven yards in a day.

Most of the farmers repair their own walls; it is one of the jobs for the month of June, the slackest time of the year for dale farmers, and the month when, if ever, they take a holiday. There is one old farmer well over seventy living not far from Muker who always goes away in June; he thinks it gives him new ideas. He does not take long journeys. Scarborough is the farthest he has been to, and sometimes he does not get beyond Richmond; but he looks forward all the year to that holiday. He is an exception, though; many of the farmers rarely leave the dale.

From the end of June until haymaking the time is taken up with shearing. Here again, as with dipping, two or three farmers help each other, so as to get the sheep back on to the moors quickly; but also because, according to the women, the men like to gossip as they work. The women often help at shearing-time by rolling up the fleeces as they are clipped off, ready for storing until the wool-buyers come round.

It is a sight in late spring in Muker to see the feather beds out for their yearly airing. In these high regions cleaning must not be started too soon, but out the beds come with the first really warm days. There must be very few hair mattresses yet in Muker. These feather beds hang over the walls, on chairs in the gardens, even out of the bedroom windows, which shut down upon them like teeth in a cream bun; other windows are taken up with pillows and bolsters. At the same time there will be a gay row of quilts hanging over the line. Even on washing days, when dusters hang over fences, rows of stockings decorate the gates, and crops of handkerchiefs appear on the bushes, the village has a festive air. But feather-bed days are much more important; they suggest work and scrubbing going on inside rooms from which those wobbling shapes have escaped for a day.

A little beyond the bridge where the beck joins the river there is a last view up that majestic valley on the north side of Kisdon, with Crackpot Hall a dark spot on the hill-side, and the gaunt slopes of Swinnergill behind it.

On the right side of the road from Muker to Gunnerside, two tracks, the first turning up at Oxnop and the second at Satron, climb the fell, and meet at the top on their way to Wensleydale. On the hill just above the road on the Oxnop track, Crow Trees, a weathered farm-house, sits with a fine, unstudied ease. Higher, the ridge of the fell ends in a limestone cliff very like a cliff on the sea coast; above it the path goes over Stony Gill Head to the moor, and then down to the ancient town of Askrigg with its old houses and church, its cross and bull ring. Walking back again, the green valley of Swaledale lies suddenly before you, its narrowness accentuated here.

Gunnerside

CHAPTER X

GUNNERSIDE, IVELET, AND THE OLD GANG MINES

BETWEEN Oxnop Gill and Satron, a lane on the left leads down to the hamlet of Ivelet. A beck runs beside it, leaping over shelves of rock to join the river. The lane narrows to go over an ancient pack-horse bridge. This highly arched bridge is one of the gems of Swaledale, a perfect specimen, unspoilt by flood or storm. It is known as the Humpbacked Bridge, and can be seen best from a footpath leading to Satron in the fields above the river.

The lane which crosses the bridge to Ivelet may have been part of the Corpse Way; there is a large stone near one end of the bridge similar to those on which the bearers are said to have rested the coffin. It is possible that the field path to Satron continued it. A generation ago, when super-stition was strong in the dale, the lane was believed to be haunted by a headless black dog which to see meant tragedy of some kind. The dog was always seen gliding on to the bridge, where it would disappear over the edge.

The cottages of Ivelet stand close under the fells at the side of a ravine down which Ivelet Beck rushes in a waterfall of three leaps, a hundred feet in length. At first sight Ivelet appears to be a sleepy little place, but this is deceptive, for its people are original. We met an old man there who, after he had talked to us for a while, said suddenly: 'Are ye interested i' old china?' He opened the door of his cottage, and stood back with a smile to watch the effect on us. The big kitchen was like a china-collector's dream. In many an antique shop there is not the choice of specimens which this man had collected. Lustre jugs hung in lavish array round the room, and there was other lustre ware, Spode, old spiral glasses, old crystal, packed on a cabinet and ranged on a sideboard, tables, and shelves round the room. Practically every piece was without a snip; broken things, even antiques, do not appeal to this ardent collector. He knows each piece perfectly, and fondles it lovingly as he brings it down, telling how this came from a farm higher up the dale, this from Wensleydale, how he picked this up at a sale in Todmorden. He has a few pieces of old furniture, a grandfather's clock, and a table, but the china and glass are the chief glory. No offer of money will tempt him to part from one of his treasures, he is very firm about that. They have taken the place of a wife and children for him. With them for company he lives happily alone in the cottage, dusting and sorting them as carefully as a woman. And this is a sturdy dalesman with a merry twinkle in his eye and a joke for all.

While we were looking at the collection a little bent woman with a sunbonnet drawn over her face, and leaning heavily on her stick, passed the door.

'Hes ta seen oor pig, fayther?' she called out in an agitated voice.

'Nay, mother,' the collector retorted.

'Whya, it's lost,' she screamed, and hurried on as fast as she could hobble.

The old man went on showing his china and glass for a few minutes as though she had never spoken, then he looked out. The woman was driving a pig out of a field at the end of the lane. We smiled at her agitation. 'It couldn't have gone far away, could it?' we asserted superiorly.

'I've kent a pig ga three mile,' the collector said, 'lowpin' anny walls or hedges that cam i' t' way.'

We believed him; but, looking at the great creature being driven towards us, we thought what a ghastly sight it would be leaping walls on its way to adventure, and felt that rather would it blaze its trail by the gaps it left in them.

The old woman came up, very relieved to have found the pig, which she explained was not hers, but her nephew's. 'He cam ter me an' he says, "Auntie, if ye're deuin' nowt, wad yer leuk efter t' pig a bit? Ah want ter cleean t' stee oot, an' oor Lizzie's gitten t' toothwark." Well, ah said ah wad, for tha're varra geud ter me; but ah jist went in yance ter leuk at fire, an' when ah cam oot pig was off. Aye, ah'se better noo, but it gav me palpitation, as it warn't me own pig, but me nevvy's.'

'Aye, mother,' said the collector, 'but I reckon ye'll be gitten a bit o' that pig sometime.'

'Aye, fayther,' she said, in exasperation. She insisted on calling the old man 'father,' but it ruffled her to be called 'mother.' 'But ah warn't thinkin' o' that. Tha're varra geud ter me, but it's their pig.'

She wandered on in silence for a time, gravely watching the bulky form heaving from side to side as it walked. Then she said, ruminatingly: 'Aye, it'll mak' a nice bit o' bacon.'

Such is the fate of most Swaledale pigs, to be 'bits o' bacon' for their owners' eating.

Gunnerside Lodge on the hill behind the hamlet is an old house which has been enlarged as a shooting-lodge for Lord Rochdale, and has taken the place of the shooting-lodge on Keld Green. From here a narrow, open road with common pasture on either side and neat cottages dotted along it runs down to Gunnerside. Farmers in Gunnerside may graze sheep and cattle on the common land. They employ a shepherd, but fetch the cows down for milking themselves.

Gunnerside, meaning Gunnar's pasture, was probably named after the Norse chief who settled there, Gunnar being a common name in Norway. The village possesses the unspoilt spirit of Swaledale. Its greyness is not depressing. It is a place of sudden changes, its houses now spreading out against the hill-side, now drawing close together in the curve of the road, now planting themselves on a steep green, a part of Gunnerside known as Lodge Green. The gill flows straight through the village.

Situated as it was in the very heart of the mining district, near to the famous Old Gang Mines, it suffered perhaps more than other villages at their closing down, and showed it in its look of ruin and desolation. But that has now vanished, partly owing to its new landlord, Lord Rochdale, and partly because of its increasing popularity with visitors. Very good fishing is to be had in the beck and river. There is one inn, 'The King's Head,' whose sign has the painting of a portly monarch with a strange resemblance to the landlord. The landlord is the son of the late proprietress, Mrs. Shaw, who died at Gunnerside in 1933, and was a famous hostess in the dale a generation ago.

The people of Gunnerside have lost the touch of lethargy which robs the dwellers in the upper dale of their enthusiasm, while they have not yet caught the sophistication of more civilized regions. Though the place is typical of Swaledale, it has many connections with the outer world. Sons and daughters, finding no work in the dale, have gone from it to London and made their mark in the world, for the dalespeople are clever if given a chance to develop. Those who leave do not forget their native place, and pass on their love for it to succeeding generations. This is especially true of the miners who went into Lancashire. In Burnley, Nelson, and other towns, annual Swaledale reunions are held, at which large numbers gather. The younger people like to come on visits to the dale, and the older ones often return to live when they have finished work.

The track to the Old Gang Mines starts on the east side of Gunnerside Beck, and turns over Melbecks Moor. Weird and lonely, it would seem that no human beings but shepherds had penetrated to these fells. Then the great scars of the Old Gang Mines appear, enormous heaps which look as though some giant mole had burrowed there, giving an almost terrifying desolation to the moor. The tippings left by 't' owd man' are softened into mounds; it will take centuries to cover the acres of barrenness which later miners have left. But the moor is too vast for even so great an upheaval to spoil; rather does the dreariness emphasize the surrounding beauty. The name Old, or Auld, Gang, from the Old English *gang*, a road, is added evidence that these mines were already old when the Saxons settled in the district in the sixth and seventh centuries.

It is said that the area known as Merryfield was so rich, that as much lead ore was taken from it as there were tippings left. Here are the ruins of Merryfield House, once a blacksmith's shop; lower down is Moor House, evidently a smallholding, for a walled field surrounds it; and lower still, on Hard Level Beck, is the tenement of Level House, which

7

had the oldest blacksmith's shop connected with the mines. In the Grinton parish registers there is an entry of the christening in 1744 of Mary, daughter of John Borras of Levell Houss, and in 1806 the christening of William, son of James Bland of Moor House, near Old Gang. These and other entries show that a small community lived round Old Gang. Miners coming from a long distance would lodge with the tenants of these houses from Monday until Saturday, bringing with them enough food for the week in wallets on their backs. 'Shops,' or 'sleeping-houses,' were also attached to the mines.

Lower down the beck, in a hollow of the moors, are the remains of the smelt-mills. Looked at from the hills they too might be a ruined village. They add to the grandness of the stretch of moor as a ruined abbey adds to the beauty of riverside meadows; and their history, if of another kind, is as interesting.

A large building of which the stone ends and pillars remain was the peat warehouse; this had a thatched roof. Peat was burnt along with hard coal in the smelting-furnaces; a year's supply could be stored in the warehouse. Coal from the King's Pit, near Tan Hill, was found to be the best for smelting purposes. The smelt-mill lies a little nearer to the beck; its four furnaces can still be seen. Four archways, A, B, C, D, stood above the furnaces, but in October 1933 these were pulled down and taken to Muker to be used in building the new Methodist chapel. In many of the smaller buildings huge bellows which were used to draw the furnaces are left to rot.

The early miners used a much more primitive kind of smelting-furnace. A circle of stone was built about two feet high in which the lead ore was placed over a fire of peat and brushwood, and at one side of which a trough was dug to carry the melted lead. These circles, known as 'bayles,'

were built on low hills facing the prevailing winds to obtain
a good draught. Beldi Hill, near Crackpot Hall, was probably used as a 'bayle hill.'

An interesting remain is the long chimney which runs
up the moor for half a mile, starting above the furnaces
and following the lie of the land. Built in the early nineteenth century of stone, it has the appearance of a level
which has made a false start and got lost outside instead of
cutting into the earth. It ends as an upright chimney on a
plateau which is still bare from the effect of its fumes. On
its way upwards the smoke clung to the sides of the chimney
and solidified. At intervals the interior was scraped and the
contents 'roasted' to extract the soot from the lead, which
afterwards went through the smelting process again.

Many deep crevices in the hills round the mines were
caused by 'hushing,' a very early method of prospecting for
and working the veins. For this process water was collected
in a dam at the top of a hill, and then turned down the hill
so that its force washed away the earth from the lead. At a
later date diviners were employed to locate the veins. Waves
of prosperity resulted in improvements and development.
More efficient ways of pumping out the water enabled the
shafts to be made much deeper. At the beginning of the
nineteenth century, when enormous profits were being
made—£60,000 was made in one year in a mine—costly
and elaborate schemes of extension were started, but the
decline in the industry came before many of them were
completed.

The men worked under conditions which would not be
allowed to-day. They descended the shafts in complete dark-
ness by ladders on either side, the last man pulling the door
to after him. In telling of it now they think it was better
to be dark, or, seeing the chasm below them, they might
have lost their nerve. To add to the danger they carried the

props fastened to leather belts which they wore round their waists; the slipping of a prop would have caused the men below to lose their footing. But there were few accidents. One man was not careful to knock all the snow from his clogs, and as he shut the door behind him he slipped and hurtled to the bottom; and a boy whose father had always carried him down begged to go alone, and he too fell to the bottom. In the Grinton registers for 1778 is this entry:

James Spensley of Smarber ⎱ Thease was Two Brothers kild in the Lead
Ralph Spensley of Blades ⎰ Mines at Old Gang.

Women and children were also employed in the mines, doing what was called 'kibbling,' washing and gathering up the bits of lead ore left in the streams and near the openings of the levels. They wore straps fixed across their shoulders to hold the buckets they carried, which were called 'kibbles.' In the seventeenth century the women who carried the ore received a shilling a week and two flannel petticoats a year. There is a cave in Westmorland called the Blue Jack Cave, where a pedlar, who was known as Blue Jack because he sold blue cloth, is said to have been murdered. The material he sold was probably that worn by women workers in the mines. As late as the beginning of the nineteenth century we are told that the women wore blue petticoats. Superstition was common among the miners, and witch stones were often hung on nails in various parts of the mine. Many of the miners walked six or seven miles to their work, and they relieved the monotony by knitting as they walked. 'Let's sit down for six needles,' was a common expression when they wanted a rest.

The lead was carried from the mills on pack-horses, later in carts, to Richmond and Barnard Castle. Even to-day the tracks along which it went are firm roads. A little below the ruins, near a bridge and a smaller smelting-mill, these tracks meet as cross-roads to Feetham, Healaugh, and

Arkengarthdale. But the workers come no more along them, and over the ruins a sad silence broods, broken only by the birds which cry unconcernedly overhead, the calls of the sheep and lambs in the spring, and occasionally the voice of a man shouting to his dogs as they catch rabbits on the hill-side near the chimney.

Pine-trees near Melbecks

CHAPTER XI

ACROSS THE VALLEY TO HARKERSIDE

THE road going up the dale from Gunnerside crosses the Swale over a bridge which slants conveniently upwards with the hill. Just below this bridge Gunnerside Beck empties itself into the river. Above it a narrow lane turns to the left to run along the hill on the south side of the river to Crackpot and Summer Lodge.

A large house on the left of the lane is Spring End, a home since Elizabethan days of the Broderick family, one of whom has the peculiar epitaph on his tomb in Muker churchyard. It is still owned by the family, though now only used as a holiday residence, and one end is a farm-house. Resting as it does close under the fells, for six months of the year the sun never reaches the back of the house. The front stands bravely up to the weather. An ancestor of the Brodericks planted two Dutch elms near the house to show his allegiance to the Orange family. Some years ago, when the interior was being altered, one of the dividing walls was found to be double, and a skeleton had been built in between; its story is unknown.

The name of the family shows them to be of Scandinavian descent, their ancestors probably coming into the dale with the Norse chief, Gunnar, who named Gunnerside. They remained for many generations yeoman farmers. Some of their descendants have had unusual ideas about their tombs and burial-places. During the last century one of them expressed a wish to be buried on a ridge of the fells behind Spring End, over which he had roamed, and which he had loved, as a boy. He died in Hawes on 28th December 1886, and from there a few days later, in bitterly cold weather, his funeral procession started out. On the Buttertubs Pass it was overtaken by a blizzard, and snow lay thickly. It was a wild journey, but the mourners struggled on, to be met at Muker by the vicar with the news that the bishop had forbidden him to read the burial service over one who had deliberately planned to be buried in unconsecrated ground. In a hailstorm, relays of bearers carried the coffin to the grave on a level terrace of the hill, and a brother of the dead man read the service. In 1932, another Broderick was buried there, but his remains were first cremated.

It is a peaceful spot, this terrace above the house, sheltered and nearly hidden by a border of birch-trees. It is known as Birk Hill. No rails or inscription mark the grave, simply a mound with a heap of stones at its head.

On the moors behind is a place known as Bloody Wall. There is an old tale of a Swaledale man named Long Tom and his sweetheart who had just parted near her home when she was seized by Scots raiders. The man raised an alarm, and the dalesmen marched to her rescue. They surprised the Scots in a hollow, and massacred them in the place since called Bloody Wall. But a Scotsman escaped with the girl, and she was never seen in the dale again.

The road past Spring End winds along the slopes of Birk Side, dipping up and down, but always rising more than it falls, until it reaches the hamlet of Crackpot, a group of houses above a wooded gill. This hamlet, which must not be confused with Crackpot Hall above Muker, gets its name from a cave in the beck above Summer Lodge, known as Crackpot Cave or Fairy Hole. The name Crackpot means a pot where crows abound, the word *pot* being Scandinavian for a deep hole. Beyond Crackpot a comparatively level road runs, at first far above the beck, but, as the ravine ends, ambles pleasantly along beside it. The ravine is beautifully wooded with hazels, sloes, and junipers. In about a mile the level stretch ends, and the hills rise sheer again; a large house under them on the right is Summer Lodge, another home of the Broderick family, now a farm.

To reach Fairy Hole you must follow the road past the farm through a gate, and then turn off it to the left through another gate. The path runs beside the beck until this is joined by a smaller one running down the hill; the cave is a few yards up this second beck. The entrance is shallow, but opens into a lofty space. Loose boulders cover the ground, which in a few yards slopes down, having the appearance of the wreck of an imposing staircase. A stone pillar stands at the bottom where water rushes out of the rock, and there are narrow passages beyond. From here the stream runs underground, and comes to the surface again just below the mouth of the cave.

The Summer Lodge road leading on to the moor is a steep track with a hairpin bend, famous for motor trials, but otherwise unfit for motors. A signpost at the top marks the ways to Askrigg, Low Row, and Reeth. The road from Askrigg to Reeth is part of a Roman way from Bainbridge to Feetham and Arkengarthdale known as the Streets. A lane leads down from the signpost to a deserted lead-mine which stands hushed and expectant as if it still listens for the workmen who never come, listens although moor grass and heather are quickly covering its tippings.

To the east the wooded glen stretches down like a serpent creeping from his mountain lair. Elsewhere all is brown moorland, as though that serpent had scorched it with his breath. To the west and north the hills of Swaledale rear themselves in a semicircle: Shunnor, lightened by a gleam of sunshine so that its currack stands out like a lone figure; Lovely Seat, retreating a little before it; and Mount Calva, crouching like a wild beast ready to spring. A grouse, hardly distinguishable from the moor, stands motionless near. This moorland was part of the great Wensleydale Forest. There are many tales of violence on the road which runs over it to Askrigg. On its summit black-headed gulls nest on the shores of Summer Lodge Tarn.

Back in the hamlet of Crackpot the road forks, and the right branch leads down Whitaside past an old mill to Melbecks. As you descend a change comes over the land-scape; it is well wooded and pine-trees line the river bank.

The stream which flows down to Melbecks is known as the Haverdale Beck. This name, coming from the Norse *halfri*, oats, suggests that in early times oats were grown in the district. Until comparatively recent days corn was grown on the level ground near the river. It has been said that the now ruined Haverdale Mill was built on the site of an ancient corn-mill; if so all signs and records of it have vanished. But there are some well-defined cultivation terraces on the slope between Ivelet and Gunnerside, showing that corn was grown here in very early days. These were flat ridges cut along the hill-side, wide enough for oxen to pull the plough; in hilly country they formed the Common Field system which lasted in remote districts later than medieval days.

A little higher up the stream there was once a small fulling-mill, to which the dalespeople brought their knitted socks, jerseys, and coats to be fulled. Up to the middle of the nineteenth century the men and women knitted incessantly in their spare time to augment their poor wages, although this work also was very badly paid. The garments were knitted much too large with unwashed, oily wool, and were then taken to the mill where they were washed and shrunk in soapy waters before being sold.

The tale of Haverdale Mill is another of achievement and decline. It was first built as a worsted-mill for making carpets; the coarse, rather harsh wool of the moorland sheep is suitable for carpets. The mill was owned by a family named Knowles who have been generous in their gifts to the dale. Edmund Knowles gave a piece of land called Broken Intake on Kisdon to the chapel at Keld, the rent of which was to go towards the salary of the minister. For years the mill, making a good quality of carpets, was successful. Then it was enlarged and new machinery was introduced. The stream was dammed higher up, but there was never enough force of water to drive the new machinery, and eventually the mill was closed. It was used for a time as a flour-mill, but, being so far from the present corn-growing districts, that too was a failure. From then, until it became too ruinous, it was used for concerts and whist-drives. Now, crumbling and roofless, it remains to show another of the lost industries of Swaledale.

Leaving Melbecks, a turning to the left over Belle Isle Bridge leads on to the main road, but the road straight on, keeping south of the river, goes along Whitaside to Harkerside Moor, whose name, from the Scandinavian *akr*, an acre or open field, seems to show that this district also was cultivated. The name of Harker, common as a family name in Swaledale, probably originated here. It was a Scandinavian custom to appropriate a place name for a family; and from *Akr* it has gradually become Harker.

But there is no sign now of arable land on Harkerside, whose lower slopes are meadow with a few farm-houses and whose higher ones are moorland. A great part of it is covered with juniper-trees. These thick, dwarfed bushes are very attractive; short as they are they have a suggestion of forest about them. At one time there were hundreds of acres of juniper-trees in Swaledale. The chips were used for fumigating during times of plague or sickness, and no house would be without them. The berries were used medicinally and as a spice. It is a shrub which grows best on high, open, limestone country.

A little way along Harkerside, an opening leads down to where an ancient ford, known as Scabba Wath, crossed the river. This was a foot-ford on the Roman road from the camps at Bainbridge to Greta Bridge; the beginnings of the stepping-stones are still there, and the cutting out of the river bank can be traced on the far side. A track would run from this ford to a ridge up Harkerside on which there is an earthwork or camp known as Maiden Castle.

From its position and arrangement it is thought that Maiden Castle was originally an early British camp, constructed as a retreat where a stand could be made against attack; and that, lying as it does near their road and midway between Bainbridge and Great Bridge, it was later taken over by the Romans and used as a halting-place. It occupies a large, irregular circle about 140 by 90 yards, and is surrounded by earthworks, below which is a deep ditch cut out of the hill on the high side and following the lie of the land on the lower. It is approached from the east by an avenue of stones, and there are piles of stones at the entrance as though there had been some kind of gateway there. Outside the entrance is a round tumulus, and an oblong tumulus stands at the west end. Tradition has it that a chest of gold lies buried under the first mound, and many have searched for it. We found an old spade on one side with its edges curled over, which might have been left by some disconsolate digger. Flint arrow-heads have been found on the surrounding moors.

It was a secure site, either as a fortress or a halting-place, with the river below and the boggy moor behind. Keen eyes would watch from this hidden ridge for figures moving over Mount Calva or along Fremington Edge beyond Reeth, another Roman way, and wonder were they friends or foes. Walking along the earthworks you try to imagine the kind of people who pitched their camp in the flat ring which they surround. The scene to-day is very different, for there is little left of the forest which the Romans saw. The village of Healaugh stands primly below with a large house among the trees in the ravine; behind it innumerable tracks cut across the moor. Lower down the valley Reeth lies snugly on its terrace under Calva.

This road along the lower slopes of Harkerside runs to Grinton, but a footpath branching down to the left by the first farm-house leads to the river, which is crossed here by a swing-bridge. Before the bridge was built, in 1920, the children going to school at Reeth from Harkerside had to cross on stepping-stones, or go round by Grinton if the river was full. A climb up the opposite hill-side brings them out on to the road near the school, just above Reeth.

The Swale near Strands

CHAPTER XII

FROM GUNNERSIDE TO REETH

THE road from Gunnerside keeps company with the river; the two may curve and twist away occasionally, but they are never far apart. More trees appear as they journey down. On the fells on either side, the same grey cottages, alone or grouped into tiny hamlets, boldly face the weather, but the stubborn, dogged character is going from the road running now along the valley.

On this stretch the first new houses appear, their fresh stone showing out from the rest. Houses have been built or enlarged higher up the dale, but nearly always of old stone, so that you do not realize their newness. It is probably economy more than taste which has brought this about. Following the new regulations for cow-sheds, there has necessarily been much rebuilding of barns; but in the upper dale the farmer, when he finds that his cow-houses have to be enlarged, looks round for a wall no longer really needed, and down it comes to reappear as part of a barn. However, with a few exceptions these new houses have been built in a style which suits the district, and the years will mellow them.

At first the hills rise steeply from the road, but at Strands there is a kind of clearing bounded by the slopes of Rowleth Wood, a paradise for spring flowers. After Belle Isle, where the bridge crosses to Melbecks, scattered houses, the beginnings of Low Row, appear.

But the slopes above the road are full of interest. You are always making discoveries in the tiny hamlets; finding, among the ruins, doorways and windows obviously not built for cottages, old burial grounds, old roads. About two miles from Gunnerside, just before a quarry and across the road from a new brick building, a barn a field's length above the road stands on the site of Smarber chapel, and is built from its stones. At its west end there is a walled enclosure with a few tombstones inside, some as recent as the nineteenth century. Grass and nettles grew thickly round them until a few years ago, when the place was cleared and taken care of. Smarber chapel was built and endowed by Philip Lord Wharton in 1691, that same Lord Wharton who left money for Bibles to be distributed to school-children who could recite certain psalms. Having become a Nonconformist, he did much for the new religion, especially for ministers who had been driven out of their churches for adopting the new views. Some of them were found other churches, and some, strangely enough, were put in charge of his lead-mines. At that time no chapel was allowed to be built within five miles of a church; Smarber is just outside that limit from Grinton.

All records of the original chapel are lost; but it was registered at the quarter sessions held at Thirsk in 1691 as a

'Meeting House adjoining Smarber Hall for Protestant Dissenters.' The first minister, the Rev. John Holland, was ordained in 1693. Lord Wharton endowed the chapel with two parcels of land in the parish of Kirkby Stephen, the rents of which are now part of the salary of the Low Row Congregational minister. In order to retain the endowment, one service a year is held outside the barn, generally on the second Sunday in August. Owing to the loss of the trust deeds, there was at one time a danger of the chapel losing the land; but in 1716 the minister's daughter married the man who was to succeed her father, and their daughter in her turn married the following minister, thus securing the ownership by over sixty years of undisputed possession. The Congregational chapel at Low Row, built in 1809, and rebuilt in 1874, took the place of Smarber chapel.

Lord Wharton's influence in the dale accounts for the strong Nonconformist element to-day. Even at the Restoration, when many people were glad to go back to the established religion, the majority of the people in Swaledale kept to the new faith in spite of persecution. A century and a half later, John Wesley had a great reception among them.

Lord Wharton had a hunting-lodge at Smarber, the remains of which are now attached to a farm which still goes by the name of Smarber Hall. They are used as a sheep-pen, sheep being dipped there. The roof has gone, but the square stone lintels of the doors and windows, and a great stone fireplace in what must have been the hall of the house, tell of its former dignity. Like Crackpot Hall, this would be built in the days of deer-hunting.

A track turning from Smarber to the moor passes through the hamlet of Blades, surprising to find so high on the fells. The cottages are grouped round a green; one of them has the inscription RF 1705 EF. IB over the doorway. This track is a continuation of the Corpse Way, and at

Riddings farm, a little farther along, there are, in a corner of a meadow, the remains of a barn known as the Dead House. Funeral processions coming from a long distance are said to have halted here for the night, the bearers leaving the coffin in the Dead House while they went down to the Punch Bowl Inn at Feetham for a merry evening. Of all the tales of the Corpse Way, that of the Dead House is the most tenacious. It and the stones along the route are proofs of its reality. From Blades the track descends into Low Row and Feetham.

Low Row spreads itself out; its cottages are dotted along the main street or in haphazard fashion up the side, with stretches of hilly green between them and the road. It merges imperceptibly into Feetham, the two making one long village. The place has lost itself a little. Its stone houses and their irresponsible placing are of the dale; but many of them are occupied by visitors and retired people, whose air of leisure has robbed the village of its own distinctive quality. Its people seem swamped by these new-comers.

In spite of this our most vivid recollection of Low Row is a sale in one of its cottages, an unsophisticated affair. The garden of this cottage turns its back sulkily on the road, but smiles down at the river. Its owner, an old lady, had died six months before, long enough for the shock of death to have gone. She had had a full life, and for that part of the world an adventurous one, and she had ended her days in that cottage above the Swale. There was pathos, but not tragedy, in the disposal of the worldly possessions which she had gathered round her, though, as if in sympathy that they were to be scattered, it rained, rained so hard that there were intervals when everyone rushed inside to shelter. During these the people went poking and prying about, the women curious to see what this other woman, who had seen and done more than they, had left behind.

The auctioneer was a young butcher, who comes up the dale once a week with a motor-van to sell meat, and in an economy of labour uses the opportunity to plaster bills of any of his sales at convenient points on the way. Many of the buyers were his customers who had come from all parts, and he treated them as friends. He seemed to know that this lady had had a few breakages in her crockery lately, that one was considering new curtains, and another had a corner needing a rocking-chair. The old lady had been a hoarder. There were innumerable bundles made up of patches of material, and there were hats, some so old-fashioned that in a few years they might have graced a pageant. The bidding for these was slow, a penny or a halfpenny being the usual prices; even then some hung fire, and had to be thrown for anyone who caught them, which made a little light relief. A high, heavily-boned pair of black stays and several odds and ends along with them the auctioneer could not sell, and at last he threw them across to the local policeman, saying: 'Here, give me a halfpenny for them, Joe; they'll make thee uniform fit well, and I'll put a hat in wi' them.' But these were mild diversions, the atmosphere on the whole was serious; sales are few and far between in the dale, and the opportunity was not to be missed or lightly passed over.

The auctioneer made one slip in the names. 'Mrs. Calvert,' he called out, when the bidding for one lot was closed. 'Nay, lad,' said the woman, 'it's miss, nut missis.' 'Well, well, so it is. Nivver mind. It's an honour to be called missis.' 'Depends wheea's missis y' are,' called a mournful voice from the back. Feather beds are in great demand at local sales, and the buses carried some bulky loads home from Low Row that day.

At Feetham there is the famous Punch Bowl Inn, a high stone building, its one note of colour the figure of Punch gaily sitting in a bowl. Until a few years ago two lead dogs

8

hung over the door, put there in memory of two dogs which chased a fox from Swaledale to the border of England and Scotland, disappearing from their masters on the way to the hound trials at Tan Hill in which they should have taken part, and returning home two or three days later. In 1929 the Punch Bowl Inn was partly burnt down; but it was rebuilt, happily in the old style. The road from the Old Gang smelt-mills comes down beside the inn. The name Feetham is derived from the old Norse *fit*, of which the dative plural is *fitjum*, and means a meadow.

Whita Bridge crosses the Swale between Feetham and Healaugh. In the meadows to the west of it are some curious mounds, the largest resembling a barrow. These were formed by the rush of water towards the end of the Ice Age cutting through faults in the rock. At one time the river forked to flow round the large mound, and made it into an island; but debris brought down by ice and water filled up the newer channel, and the current went back to the old one. Long centuries after, some early race, finding the Howe, entrenched and terraced it, and made it into a fort.

A little past Whita Bridge is the other approach to Scabba Wath, the ford below Maiden Castle. From here it is about a quarter of a mile to Healaugh. The name Healaugh comes from the Saxon *heah*, meaning a high forest clearing; you can imagine dense forest over all this region. To-day only the ravine of Barney Beck is thickly wooded, presenting a vivid contrast to the fells beyond. This was a district famous for its deer-hunting. Lord Wharton had another hunting-lodge here named Park Hall, on the site of which there is now a farm. It was a vast estate, the name of which must not be confused with another of the Wharton estates, Healaugh—between York and Wetherby in the West Riding.

Healaugh was famous for hunting in very early days,

wolves and wild boars being chased as well as deer. In the reign of Stephen the estate was given to the Gant family, who later, probably in John of Gaunt's time, built a hall, a chapel and a lead-covered 'touresse' from which to watch the hunting in Healaugh Park. Nothing of either building remains to-day, except some mounds in a field called Hall Garth, and a ridge which marks part of the surrounding wall. A barn in some fields in the direction of Barney Beck stands on the site of John of Gaunt's stables. We learnt this from an old farmer who was very puzzled when we asked about the castle, until we mentioned John of Gaunt. 'Oh, Johnny Gaunt!' he said; 'why, them barns over there used to be Johnny Gaunt's stables.'

There is a house on the hill behind with the brave name of Dagger Stones. Near it is another ruin with lintels and doorways somewhat resembling those at Smarber, which seems to have some history behind it, but at present is not safe to explore.

Healaugh village has a peaceful, but rather mournful air, as though it remembered former greatness, and harboured just a little discontent. It seems slightly alien in Swaledale. The road goes primly and sedately from it, until it drops down the hill to Reeth.

Reeth Bridge

CHAPTER XIII

REETH AND ARKENGARTHDALE

REETH, the capital of middle Swaledale, possesses all the characteristics of the upper dale. Below it the wildness immediately gives place to the softness of the lower dale. Its position, on a terrace of the lower slopes of Mount Calva, is unique. Steep roads lead into it from higher up, and drop down from it to Fremington; yet it has no feeling of clinging precariously to the hill. Rather can you imagine that long ago Reeth came exploring up the dale, and found this flat piece of land which fitted it, and stayed there. It seems to smile, as though pleased with life. Lead industries may wane, sheep-rearing hardly pay its way, but it has for ever that lovely plateau on the hills.

Its green gives quietness as well as space. A hush falls over the village as footsteps which echoed noisily along the road turn suddenly on to the grass. A large house looks down on it from the north side, and High Row shuts it in on the west. From it you look across the valley of the Arkle to the ridge of Fremington Edge with its limestone scars and dappling of juniper-trees, and down to where the village of Grinton nestles round its ancient church.

Again, Reeth is at the foot of Arkengarthdale, the only large tributary dale running into Swaledale. It belongs to Arkengarthdale as much as to Swaledale; indeed the town actually stands on the Arkle Beck, the river having followed the slope of Harkerside to Grinton. This position gave it importance in the mining days. Its popularity to-day can be judged by the number of cars which line the green on a Sunday. Then walking tourists avoid Reeth, setting out early for the hills and forgetting this alien influx; except when from some high point they see them as black specks on the green. On other days the houses of Reeth look from the heights to be sitting round a table.

Reeth has sold a morsel of its soul for this motoring element. Some of the shops round the green, in catering for its patronage, have lost that dale atmosphere which the shops higher up possess. But you forget the motorists when the last horn has blown at the bend, and Reeth settles down to be itself again. And for many months of the year it is itself all the time.

In olden days a different bustle pervaded the town. In 1695 a charter was granted to Philip Lord Wharton, to hold a market there every Friday and four fairs a year, for buying and selling 'all manner of cattle, goods, and merchandise.' An Agricultural Show is now held in September.

In 1780 three Quaker brothers, George, Leonard, and John Raw, built and endowed a Friends' school at Reeth. Its site is marked by paving-stones on a lane which branches from the lower end of the town. The County Council school which has replaced it is still known as Reeth Friends' school.

The road to Arkengarthdale runs by the side of the Buck Hotel. There is a freedom and openness about this dale which is attractive after the narrowness of Swaledale. The road which sweeps up it gives again the sense of adventure. At first it is just an open road over the fell, with moorland on either side, and a single telegraph-wire beside the road. At the top of the rise an expanse of valley stretches out, and the road tugs impatiently, like an eager child urging you to hurry to the beauties to which it leads.

Arkengarthdale has not the romantic beauty of Swaledale. This district which was once all forest is, except at Eskeleth, now very sparsely wooded, nor have its scarred hills the grandeur of the bigger dale. It had the most important lead-mines after the Old Gang, and, though white farm-houses and cottages dot its hill-sides, a faint atmosphere of the industrial still hangs over its villages. Mine-tippings mar the fells, and ancient levels look out from them like black windows.

Arkil, the son of Gospatrick, held this estate before the Conquest, and gave his name to the valley, calling it 'Arkil's garth,' the valley of Arkil's enclosure. Other names indicate the early settlement of the dale. Booze, high up on the hill-side to the right, means the house by the bow or curve, the curve being either Arkle Beck which flows below it, or Slee Beck which runs at the side of it. Its name in 1473 was Bowe-house, which has gradually changed to Booze, most inappropriately, for it does not possess an inn. It is a forgotten place with a neglected road leading to it. There is a fine walk from it over the moor to Hurst.

A path through the woods below Booze comes out at Arkletown, the first village up the valley, a place which has yielded its importance to Langthwaite, a mile higher up the dale. Even its church has gone. The foundations were undermined by the Arkle Beck, and a new church was built at Langthwaite in 1818. Nothing is left of the old building but its graveyard, with forlorn-looking tombstones, bent at all angles.

About half a mile above Langthwaite is the C.B. Inn, called after Charles Bathurst, Esq., Lord of the Manor in the eighteenth century, who opened out many new lead-mines, and whose initials were stamped on the pigs of lead. The Bathurst family owned Arkengarthdale for generations. In 1628, the citizens of London sold the estate to Dr. John Bathurst, physician to Oliver Cromwell. Dr. Bathurst, who had been head master of Richmond Grammar School until 1631, left money in his will to found a grammar school in Arkengarthdale. His descendants developed the mining industry in this dale as the Denys family did in Swaledale.

The C.B. Inn lies at the point where the turnpike road crosses the Roman road which forded the Swale at Scabba Wath, near Maiden Castle, and has since cut over the west of Calva. After passing the inn it ran across the north edge of Windegg Moor, and along the present road over the Stang to Barnard Castle. The road was used by the Romans for transporting lead from the Arkengarthdale mines.

About a quarter of a mile above the inn the present road to Barnard Castle branches off to the right. The C.B. Mines are a little higher, on the hill to the left. The ruins of the smelt-mills stand below them near the road. The most interesting building is an older smelt-mill in the middle of a field on the lower side of the road. Octagonal in shape, it has the appearance of a tithe barn. In its huge interior, now used for storing, carts and reapers look lost. The original beams support the roof, and there are remains of the furnaces; but most of the inside has been taken out, and the stone from it used to build four cottages. Old mining tools can still be found, buried in the earth on the floor. The wind moans and whistles through the empty windows. The building was disused even in the prosperous days of mining, when the new smelt-mill nearer to the mine was built. The remains of the chimney of this later smelt-mill, two and a half miles long, can still be traced. A smaller building on the low side of the road was a blasting-mill, used for storing powder, but for this too another mill was eventually built in a safer place higher up the fell. The C.B. Setts with the Surrender Pit at the Old Gang Mines linked up thirty miles of lead-mines.

At their zenith the C.B. Mines employed between two and three hundred men. In 1909 an attempt was made to work them again; but, like that at the Old Gang Mine, it was a failure. During the experiment, a gentleman named Morley Alderson, hearing of it, wrote to Mr. Thomas Harker, the manager, telling that his great-uncle, Sir George Douglas Alderson, had leased the mines along with Peter Denys, and how the two men travelled up from London four times a year by coach and post-chaise, the journey taking six to seven days. In the letter he refers to an old rhyme:

> When Julius Cæsar was a king,
> Bowes Castle and Hurst and Arkendale
> Mines was a famous thing.

The quarrying of chert is now carried on in Arkengarthdale. This is a hard, flint-like stone which is ground into a whitish powder and used for making china. But the chert quarries here only employ about sixteen men.

The road dips sharply to the tiny hamlet of Eskeleth on the opposite slope. A barn here shows obvious signs of having been a chapel, though most of the interior has gone. It is reminiscent of that at Raven Seat, but it belonged to a small sect called the Barkerites, followers of a man named Barker who broke away from the existing church. Here at Eskeleth the mining tradition seems to cling; the ruins are always there as a reminder.

A mile above, another road turns down to Whaw, the last village in Arkengarthdale, nestling under the round-topped Kitlaw Hill with pine-trees surrounding it on all

sides. The three-arched stone bridge which spans the beck
here gives a feeling of age, and incidentally shows by its
length and height that the Arkle Beck which it crosses is
not always a gentle stream. Its name, coming from the old
Norse *kui*, has had curious changes, being in 1280 Kiwawa,
in 1285 le Kuawe, and in 1342 Quagh. It has the lovely
meaning of 'an enclosure near the fold where sheep are
milked.' The meaning of Kitlaw, 'the hill near the cow
valley,' also from the old Norse, suggests almost a dairy-
farming district. At Whaw the Arkle Beck turns from a deep
hollow up which it can be tracked to its source on Water
Crag. Here habitation ceases, and the road strikes out on to
the moor. Higher up a track turns off to Bowes; but the main
road goes on to Tan Hill and down to Barras.

It is an even better walk down Arkengarthdale than up
it; the sudden line between the moor and the cultivated land
is seen more vividly this way. The villages and farms are
spread along the valley like a toy country. After days of
exploring in this dale of the Arkle you wish to go on.

Some quaint wills are preserved in *The Wills of the Manor
Court of Arkengarthdale*. One, dated 1756, reads: 'Wife Anne
for life the bed wherein we now lie, and 10s. a year when my
son Francis comes at age if she remains my widow, and if
not to have 1s. paid and Turn Out. Francis Gill of High
Green. Miner.' Another man leaves 'a little tea table and
a hanging kubbert and husbandry working tools.' In 1799
one man left 'a large seeing glass'; another, 'a pannel chest
and a Line-wheel'; and another, 'a toorse Feather bed.'
Very many of the wills exclude the wife if she marries again.

Back at Reeth the road leaves the town to cross the Arkle
over a three-arched bridge. At Fremington it passes Draycott Hall, until recently the home of Sir Francis C. E. Denys,
Bart., the owner of the mines. A statue of Saturnus seated on
a pedestal of lead in front of the house was placed there to

commemorate the inheritance of the royalties of the mines in the manors of Healaugh and Muker by Miss Anna Draycott from the sister of Lord Wharton. The present owner of the royalties does not draw a penny from them.

Beyond Draycott Hall the old road to Richmond turns off to the left, and another track starts by some white cottages up the side of Fremington Edge to Hurst. Here you meet the workers coming down from the chert-quarries on Fremington Edge. Seeing them, you can imagine those other miners, more in number, coming down from their work in the depth of the hills.

There are traces of an ancient entrenchment here, crossing the valley and proceeding parallel with the earthworks on Harkerside. Darlington Museum has some arrow-heads and a stone plough found among them, presented by the late Mr. Tom Ward. There are also in York Museum some silver-plated horse-harness and bronze articles found here, which are thought to have belonged to a travelling artisan, and to be Roman.

Fremington is a link between the town of Reeth and the village of Grinton. It tones down a little the contrast between the two.

The Cathedral of the Dales

CHAPTER XIV

GRINTON AND THE CORPSE WAY

No toning down can quite take away the suddenness of the change from Reeth to Grinton. Only half a mile from each other, so near across the valley that it seems as though a stone hurled from the green at Reeth might hit the church tower at Grinton; yet Reeth belongs absolutely to the upper dale with its storms and hardships, and Grinton to the gentler lower dale with its ancient history, and the gracious buildings which testify to it.

When the 'Domesday Book' was compiled the country beyond Grinton was said to be waste, and from there the survey turned over the moors towards Wensleydale. Its name, meaning 'a green enclosure,' shows it to have been a cultivated spot in the midst of fells and forest. To-day, while much of the surrounding waste has gone, there is that same line of difference. Its cottages climbing up to the moor have a look of age, and an architecture of which there is only a suspicion higher up the dale.

Just beyond the bridge over the Swale, and opposite the Bridge Hotel, are the remains of Blackburn Hall, a romantic-looking building with massive chimneys and stone-mullioned windows. Except for one corner which is used as a country cottage, the building is a ruin. It rests under the shadow of the church, between it and the river. The Blackburn family who owned it had the south chapel in the church.

This and Swale Hall, the home of the Swale family who owned the estate soon after the Conquest, and of which we shall say more, were the real homes of these families. The larger houses and castles, of which traces are left in the upper dale, were hunting-lodges, to which the men came to indulge in a sport which had much of the barbaric about it. But here where the nobler families lived for the greater part of the year, their influence on the people and the buildings is felt.

But the chief civilizing factor in Grinton for nearly nine centuries has been its church, the mother church even of Marrick Priory, and the first building of any architectural value in the dale. In the days when Grinton was an important market town having two fairs a year, its market was held on a Sunday so that people coming long distances could attend the services in the church and do their marketing on the same day. But whereas Muker church has come down to the people and become as one of them, Grinton, though it has not held aloof, has kept an aristocratic dignity. Its age and beauty have caused it to be known as the 'Cathedral of the Dales.'

The first church was probably an early Norman structure, though it has been thought that in pre-Conquest days, when Grinton belonged to the Saxon parish of Catterick, there was a heathen temple here which, after Paulinus came and preached and converted the people, baptizing them in the

River Swale, would be replaced by a Christian church. All that is left of the Norman building is the north jamb of the chancel arch with its scalloped capital, a small window over the tower arch, and the bowl of the font. The late twelfth-century tower arch was retained when the tower was reconstructed in 1500. The south aisle, added in the fourteenth century, and the north aisle and chapel in the fifteenth, were, apart from the arcades, rebuilt and widened in the sixteenth century. To this last period belong the south chapel, which is cut off from the nave by a sixteenth-century screen, and a little vaulted sacristy north of the sanctuary.

The north chapel was dedicated to the Swale family. It has an old wooden lectern with a chained copy of *Burkitt on the New Testament* (1752), one of the few chained books in Yorkshire. There are traces in the south chapel of a small piscina, and at the south-west corner, a curiously placed squint looks from the churchyard on to the altar. In its east window ancient glass portrays 'St. George and the Dragon,' with a bearded saint above, and the inscription, 'Maria Bredlyngtoun(e),' below. Grinton formed part of the original endowment of Bridlington Priory.

The church was restored in 1896, when many ancient relics, in use when the floor stood at a much lower level, were discovered: a large piscina in the south aisle, the west part of the sedilia in the chancel, which has been cut into by the arch of the south chapel, and a stone staircase, which led to a rood-loft, winding through the north pier of the chancel arch. Its treasures seem unending; the Jacobean pulpit, dated 1718, the font with an oak canopy reaching to the roof and supported by four clustered pillars, more ancient glass, old gravestones, one on the floor being that of Elizabeth Blackburn, buried there in 1688. In the Decorated porch grooves can be seen in the stone, made by the sharpening of arrow-heads.

Later generations added the Debased work, chiefly windows, and the flat roof, features which have impressed upon the dignity of the building a local character very fitting in that place. Yet one would not have a whit more local character. It is good to come down from the fell villages, and, stepping into the church for awhile, be uplifted by its lofty beauty. Doing so you realize the power of a religion which made men build their churches so finely, and which to-day can carry them above trivial, everyday things, so that sorrow and difficulties are forgotten for a time.

The registers of the church date from 1640. It is surprising to find in them how many people were drowned in the river and the becks. There is an interesting entry for June 25th, 1721: 'Sara Lonsdale of Healey. Haveing been brought up in ye Errors of Quakeing was baptized when she was about 50 yrs old.'

A heavy border of yews running round the churchyard at Grinton was badly damaged in the snow of 1933. These yews seem to gather round as if to protect the church from the storms which sweep down the dale. There is a feeling of age and history in the burial-ground; it has gathered to itself from the bounds of a great parish so many sons and daughters of the dale. The grey church tower seems to call its children, the wide aisles on either side to stretch out sheltering arms, and the battlemented clerestory behind to offer security. The church gazes up the dale as it did long centuries ago, watching for those slow processions down the old Corpse Way.

In some characteristics the Corpse Way seems to have resembled the old 'church-ways,' roads leading to the church; but there is no record concerning the superstition generally attached to the church-ways, that if the dead were taken any other way they would not rest in their graves

It was probably the best track from the upper dale to Grinton, which had the nearest consecrated burial-ground; and funeral processions with their burden would naturally take the easiest way. It would be used as a corpse way from the time of the first church at Grinton until the church at Muker was built, and the burial-ground consecrated, in 1580. Here and there on the route, slabs of stone about six feet long are found, on which the coffin is said to have been placed when the bearers needed a rest; the corpse was carried in a wicker basket to make the burden as light as possible. The journey from near the head of the dale often took two days.

Starting from Keld the procession would turn down the first lane to the left and over Skeb Skeugh Beck, then mount the slopes of Kisdon past the ruined cottage, making for the top to avoid the limestone crags, but choosing the easiest way through a dip in the hill. There were two stones for resting the coffin on Kisdon. Once over the top the way winds down to Muker, but takes a sudden turn to the left before reaching the village, and makes for the Carrs and the bridge leading on to Ivelet Moor, though in those days the river would be forded here. Then along the low slopes of Ivelet Moor, past Calvert Houses, and up to where Gunnerside Lodge now stands.

From here there were probably two distinct routes. One turned down to Ivelet and over the Hump-backed Bridge, then by an old track to Gunnerside where it forded the beck and the river, and proceeded along Harkerside to Grinton. The more definite way followed the road down to Gunnerside instead of Ivelet, turned on to the fells behind the village till it reached the Dead House above Low Row, then went through Feetham, Kearton, and Healaugh to Grinton. Some points in the route are uncertain, but it is easier to imagine if you realize that much of the present road was not there, and that early tracks followed the hills to avoid marsh-land and forest, which might be impassable or harbour wild beasts or robbers.

At a later date, Grinton was affected by the law which made it compulsory to bury people in wool. In 1692, Adam Barker of Level House, Old Gang, was fined £5 for burying his daughter in linen. The warrant against him, issued by the High Sheriff of the parish of Grinton, read:

Whereas information has been given to me by Ralph Elliot of Healey, that Ann Barker, daughter of Adam Barker, of Level House, near the Old Gang, was buried in Linnen contrary to the statute in that case provided. These are therefore to will and require you to levey upon the goodes and chattles of the said Adam Barker the sum of Five Pounds, half wherof is to be distributed amongst the poor of the said Parish whare she the said Ann Barker dyed, and the other half to be given to Ralph Elliot, the informer. Faill not at your perill. Given under my hand and seal the second day of May, in the year of our Lord God, 1692.—JOHN HUTTON.

In 1138 Walter de Gant, the same de Gant who held the manor of Healaugh, a kinsman of William the Conqueror, gave to the Priory Church at Bridlington the manor of East Grinton which contained Grinton Church; and to his nephew, Alured de Swale, the son of his sister Alice and John de Swale, the manor of West Grinton which contained all the lands belonging to the township of Reeth. From this Alured the family of Swale descended, apparently taking their name from the river which flowed through their lands. Here they built the manor house of Swale Hall, a little above the river on the lane which runs along the south side of the church to Harkerside.

The family played a prominent part in English history. William, the grandson of Alured, accompanied Richard Cœur de Lion to the Holy Land where he died. He was succeeded by his brother, whose grandson took part in the Scottish wars of Edward II and Edward III; he commanded a troop of archers from the dale at the Battle of Neville's Cross. In 1660 Solomon Swale, Member of Parliament for Aldborough, near Boroughbridge, proposed the restoration of Charles II in the House of Commons. In consideration of his services in the Stuart cause he was made a baronet, and received a gift of two thousand pounds from the king, and, to compensate him for his losses, the loan of another two thousand pounds to be repaid in yearly instalments at the rate of a hundred pounds a year without interest. He left a very lengthy and interesting will.

For several centuries the Swale family omitted to claim their manorial rights, and a later Sir Solomon Swale had the Crown lease of his estate and lead-mines fraudulently taken from him by a clerk in the Exchange Office who had discovered the lapse. Sir Solomon spent all his money in lawsuits to recover them, and finally died broken-hearted in the Fleet prison for debtors in 1773. The title was not resumed until 1877. With the failure of Sir Solomon Swale to get back his estates they and the house passed out of the family. In 1786 Swale Hall was sold by auction at the King's Head Hotel, Richmond, and became a farm-house.

The house stands boldly on a rise of the hill, a stone building, now unfortunately covered with stucco; but the window-mullions and some of the out-buildings, which must at one time have been part of the house, remain untouched. It has a central chimney-stack; and the original wooden bolt is still on the door. The hall where the family sat is a spacious room with a massive fireplace. From a smaller room on the other side of the door the staircase goes up between walls. Its stone steps are worn into hollows by the feet of many generations. The whole of the top story was once a single room.

On the hill-side between here and Grinton there are the remains of ancient earthworks.

A steep hill climbs up through Grinton village, and comes suddenly out on to the moor. On the left is Grinton Lodge, the shooting-lodge of Col. A. H. Charlesworth. A track to the right curls off to Redmire. John Wesley had his horse bogged here while riding from Low Row to Wensleydale in 1774.

The road straight over the moor goes to Leyburn in Wensleydale. It is a fine way from which to enter Swaledale. Starting from Leyburn, it runs past a new army camp and on to the moor. Gradually the hills of Wensleydale vanish, and those of Swaledale and Arkengarthdale appear. There is more colour on the moors here than in any part of the dale. Presently the green valley of Arkengarthdale stretches out like a promised land; and there is a glimpse of Swaledale, winding round to the left, just enough to set you longing for its upland regions. Beyond Mount Calva rise other hills, faint in the distance. Below it the trees grow thicker through Grinton to the ruins of Marrick Priory. Suddenly in the silence the mother church of the priory strikes the hour, very quickly, as though it said how small a space of time an hour was in Grinton's long story.

Marrick Priory

CHAPTER XV

THE PRIORIES OF ELLERTON AND MARRICK, AND ON
TO HURST

THE Priories of Ellerton and Marrick lie within a mile of each other, but on opposite sides of the river. It is as though the nuns came up the valley looking for a site on which to build their church and home, and wandered on and on entranced by every new turn of the way, until they saw the hills rise higher and bleaker beyond Grinton, and were afraid to go farther.

It is best to see Ellerton first. Always a more humble establishment than its sister higher up the dale, it is to-day a more humble ruin. At Grinton you are well on the way. Passing Marrick on the left, the tower of Ellerton is soon seen rising up in a field. Leland calls it a 'Priori of White Clothid Nunnes'; Whitaker 'one of the humblest of all monastic foundations.' We are told that the inhabitants were few and chiefly drawn from the most respectable families in the neighbourhood. College Close in Richmond marks the site of a training-school for this nunnery. The very land on which it stands seems more exposed than most priory sites, but in those days the country round was forest. In this lonely place the Cistercian nuns would live in silence.

The ruins are now enclosed in the grounds of Ellerton Lodge which stands close by. The *Gentleman's Magazine* for 1828 tells how an additional room was required by the owner of the lodge for the shooting-season, and workmen were told to use the stone from the church, the foundations of the cloisters and other parts. Complaints of this vandalism were made, only to be answered by the workmen's remarks that the sods had been preserved, and they would lay them down again as smooth as a bowling-green. While clearing away the rubbish two stone coffin-lids were found, and one was accidentally broken in two. These were made of lime-stone from the surrounding moors, and were in such good condition that it is thought they must have been built into the south wall, then at a lower level, not the floor. One, thought to have covered the grave of the founder, has an engraved cross and the inscription, HIC IACET WIMERUS P'SONA, in old Lombardic lettering down the sides. The other has a similar cross, but at the bottom is a triangle with an open book engraved on it and the words PETRONILE PRIORISE engraved on the leaves. Petronila was a prioress not known of before the discovery of the tombs; she died in 1251.

Ellen, another prioress whose tomb is at Ellerton, died in 1268. These two slabs, along with others, have been placed inside what remains of the walls of the nave, where grass and moss quickly fill in the engraved crosses and inscriptions. The fifteenth-century tower, still intact, looks down upon these stones as it has always done, for it stood inside the church.

The Scots, on one of the many raids which they made into Swaledale after the Battle of Bannockburn, entered this little priory and took away several charters and writings. Characteristically, at the Dissolution, Ellerton was surrendered 'without murmure or griefe' by Johanna, the last prioress.

To reach Marrick you must turn back along the road to Grinton, and over a stile on the right leading through a field to the river. Once at the river a call will bring the people from the farm-house near the priory, who have a boat which they haul across by ropes and pulleys fastened to trees on either side, an ingenious contrivance. Until this boat was fixed another farmer kept in order some stepping-stones, which were there in the time of the priory; now the river is gradually washing them away.

From the river, Marrick tower, rising protectively above the old farm-house, has a look of strength and power, but once near it, you feel most its tranquillity, as though the nuns had shed their gentleness over it for all time. The ancient ruins accentuate the beauty of the place; its stones take upon themselves the humour of the day, showing white in the sunshine and grey when the skies are clouded. Fine trees stand beside it, rising even from the ruins, and the hillside under which it shelters is thickly wooded. From its pleasant site it looks up to the grey town of Reeth, with Mount Calva and the narrow valley beyond, and, a field's length away, the river makes continual music.

Marrick Priory was founded 1154-81 by Roger de Aske for Benedictine nuns. When it was surrendered to the king's commissioners in 1539 it had a prioress and twelve nuns. The church was also the parish church of Marrick, a mile away on the hill behind, though whether it or the nunnery came first seems uncertain. The parishioners entered the church by the north door and sat in the nave, and the nuns by the south door from the cloisters and sat in the choir. The nave of the priory church was used for services until 1811, when, with the exception of the tower, it was pulled down and rebuilt with a disregard for beauty and fitness, which entirely lost its character. Old gravestones were broken up and built into the walls; one of the thirteenth-century arches was used with parts of others to form a chancel arch. The Jacobean pulpit and some interesting tombs remain. A new chapel-of-ease has now been erected in Marrick village, and the priory church is only used for funerals and a few services in the summer. Its damp walls and floor speak of decay, a neglect of something no longer vitally necessary.

It is from the few ruins beyond the church that the beauty and grace of the abbey can be imagined. In the remains of the choir and chancel there are portions of the lovely tracery of a Decorated window and another window, a trefoiled piscina, the head of a sedilia on the south, and an aumbry on the east, walls. These are now only a foot above the ground. The farm opposite may have been part of the priory. Its farm-buildings lean familiarly against the church, which stands in the midst of it, watching the life of the farm-yard as once it watched the life of the nunnery.

The calm and peace which is so attractive in Marrick must have been felt deeply in that earlier, more dangerous age in which the priory flourished. There is a story of a lady who fled there from the dissipated life of the Court of Henry VIII. Her name was Isabella Beaufort, and at the age of nineteen she was one of Queen Catherine's maids of honour, about the time that Henry was seeking to divorce the queen and marry Anne Boleyn. She was very beautiful and accomplished, and Henry was not so absorbed in Anne that he could ignore this new arrival. At last the girl, becoming terrified, dressed herself as a page, and fled from the Court. She dare not go to her home lest her parents should suffer when Henry discovered that they had taken her in, nor let the man she was in love with know where she was.

After a long and frightening journey, she arrived at Marrick Priory, worn out with fatigue. The porter, seeing a page-boy, refused to let her in, and she fainted on the doorstep. This presented a problem for the nuns, but at last in pity they carried her in to where no man but the Father Confessor had ever entered. When they found out their mistake and heard her story she was allowed to stay, though she took no vows. A few years later rumours went round the country that the monasteries and abbeys were to be dissolved, and Joan Darrell, Prioress of Amesbury in Wiltshire, came up to Marrick to discuss with its prioress what should be done. Immediately she recognized Isabella Beaufort, and, on returning home, she informed her nephew of her whereabouts, knowing that he had been in love with the girl. After that the two communicated with each other, and when the Dissolution came they were married.

You can imagine Isabella Beaufort wandering about the priory grounds. Even in her unhappiness, the tranquil atmosphere, a contrast to the life of the Court, must have soothed her. Perhaps she crossed the river over the stepping-stones below the priory to visit the nuns at Ellerton, for the white nuns there were allowed to communicate with the black-robed ones at Marrick.

A stone 'causey' runs from the priory through the wood to Marrick village with three hundred and seventy-five steps which were there in the days of the nunnery. In heat and snow it must have been a tiring way for the villagers to toil from church, but for us there is romance in treading the way they and the nuns trod. The path goes through a field and over a stile into the wood, where there is a last view of the ruins. Through the wood the path crosses a pasture into the village of Marrick. Here the trees are out of sight, open country rolls down again, and the priory seems to belong to another land. So quickly can Swaledale change its character.

Marrick seems to have taken a sensible view of things, and decided that with all the space around it would give itself room to stretch. You realize the wisdom of this and the dignity it has gained, but it gives a first impression of aloofness after the clustering habits of the higher villages. It was affected like other places with the decay of the lead industry, but it has turned, without the aid of visitors, into a farming village with spacious houses. Older people will tell how this house was once three, that barn two 'livings.' The same lot has befallen the more important dwellings; its ancient Manor House and its Vicarage have become farm-houses. Marrick and Grinton are now under one vicar.

The Vicarage stood down a lane at the extreme end of the village. The vicar did not mind the long walk through Marrick and down the steps to his church while he was a young man, but 'when he grew older it was farther away,' as an old man in the village put it. The tale is told of how he used to send his son down to see if anyone was coming to early communion, with instructions to ring a bell when he saw them begin to descend the steps. If he heard the bell the old man knew he must hurry, but if it did not ring he slept on in comfort.

The chapel-of-ease was originally built by the Roman Catholics. The Wesleyan chapel, just opposite, was erected twenty years later in 1878. The Wesleyans seem to have had an objection to their neighbours, the Catholics, for one night in their zeal they broke into the church, hauled out the pulpit, and threw it into the river. The Roman Catholic church was sold when the congregation had dwindled to one.

There are very few children in the village, so that the school has been closed, and the children are taken by bus to Reeth. The only inn, 'The White Horse,' has a painted sun-dial over the door. A hollow beam in its kitchen is made into lockers and cupboards.

An old man of eighty-nine, still alert and genial, lives at Marrick. He has been a gardener, and chuckles to think of how he has labelled the roses in his own garden with numbers only, a retort in his retirement to those ladies who, coming to inspect the roses, pulled out the labels to find their names, and put them back again in the wrong place.

The road out of Marrick joins the old Richmond to Reeth road, and crossing it goes down to Hurst where the Roman pig of lead was found. Its ancient beginnings have cast a glamour over the name of Hurst. It is one of those places which one hears of, and unconsciously imagines. The reality is a rude awakening, for Hurst is a broken village, left bewildered, its reason for being gone. It too is long and straggling, but it has not the grace and dignity of Marrick. There are ruins everywhere, and the houses which are left intact seem to weep with them. It is the only village in Swaledale which has kept its thatched roofs; at one time many of the houses in the dale were thatched. Speaking of Grinton and Richmond in the sixteenth century, Leland says: 'The houses of these two touns be partly slatid, partly thakkid.' The thatches were of ling, and as one covering wore thin another was placed on the top, until the roofs became so heavy that the beams gave way. These roofs, sagging and hanging dejectedly over the edges, add to the gloom of Hurst. One cottage has tried to rise above circumstance by painting its walls white, but this emphasizes the desolation.

Of all the Swaledale villages this only is built close up to the mines, looking on to them as a modern colliery village does. The other villages would have grown up had there been no mines, but this became a village because of them. The hill-side has been tossed and tumbled like the moors behind the Old Gang, and two now useless chimneys rise from the wreckage like tombstones. Hurst should be seen if only to realize again what the dale has lost. Time will cover the scars as it has covered the earlier ones, and only mounds remain to tell of what was once the life and meaning of the place.

A track which the miners used turns at the end of the village over the moor to Fremington Edge and Reeth, three miles away. On this healthy moorland where heather and grass-covered hills roll gently on all sides the mines and their scars are soon forgotten. But to proceed down the valley there is a route over the hills to Marske, for which a path turns to the right just beyond the inn; an easily lost path which comes out on a ridge overlooking a flat hollow. This is the site of a lake formed in the Ice Age by the rush of water from the Teesdale valley. The road from here drops down through Skelton—two or three cottages and an old hall which was started and never finished, though part of it is now made into smaller houses.

At a cottage here, three children ran to the wall to watch us pass. 'We're always weeden', we're weeden' all day,' one little boy said, very gently. And we looked and saw that the valley we had entered was rich and luxuriant, where everything, including the weeds, grew riotously.

Marske

CHAPTER XVI

MARSKE AND THE ROADS TO RICHMOND

MARSKE is 'smothered wi' trees,' indeed, as the daleswoman said. These trees are not a part of an old forest, but were planted by Mr. John Hutton, the lord of the manor at the beginning of the last century; some of those in the hall grounds are rare varieties. Mr. Hutton also tried, but with little success, to reclaim some of the moorland. Ridges made by the plough can still be seen on the moor, though covered with heather again.

Much of the history of Marske has to do with the Hutton family who acquired the manor in 1596, and still own the estate, though they do not now live in the hall. Matthew Hutton who bought the estate for his son was Archbishop of York, and a later Matthew Hutton, born at Marske, became Archbishop of York in 1747. The obelisk on the hill to the west of the village covers the grave of another Matthew Hutton who died in 1814. He had a racing-stable

near, and the horses were exercised on the hill. Marske
people say that he asked to be buried where he could hear
the tramping of the horses.

Resting in its hollow, Marske seems a soft, dreamy place.
This is deceptive, for its woods end abruptly in the moors
which still surround it. A single-arched thirteenth-century
bridge crosses the beck. An old corn-mill which stood near
it was pulled down towards the end of the nineteenth
century when the Hall grounds were altered. Above it is the
church, its walls and bell-turret hidden by trees. There was
a Norman church here, but of this only the south door and
traces in the nave remain. The nave arcade is Early English,
but the church was practically rebuilt in the seventeenth
century in a very crude manner. The font, dated 1663, the
gift of Timothy Hutton, is of the same rough work. Judging
by old accounts, the church was badly in need of restoration.
One says:

> The Seates of their church are very undecent and unfitt, and the floore
> of their church unpaved, and the church yeard (un) walled, and that they have
> the school taught in the church. They want two bookes of Homilies, a decent
> place for the minister to read prayers in, a poor man's box, and two locks
> and keep for the chest. They want pottes of pewter for the wine at Com-
> munion and a table containing the degrees of marriage.

Marske lies on the old road from Richmond to Reeth;
this was the main thoroughfare until the new road on the
other side of the river was made about the middle of the
nineteenth century. There are remains of mines round it,
but its chief share in the industry was the transport of lead
on ponies from the mines to Richmond.

Lanes and paths branch out in all directions. A wide lane
goes past the post office and the day school to Clints, sheltered by woods and high cliffs. The ancient Manor House
of Clints was pulled down when the estate and that of
Skelton were added to Marske in 1842, and the hamlet is
now only a cluster of cottages and the church Sunday school.

Beyond it the path goes deeper into the wood. In the very heart of the wood there is a clearing, and some buildings and a row of beehives appear; behind them a long garden leads up to a gamekeeper's cottage, a tall cottage which tries to peer over the trees shutting it in on all sides. It is a fascinating place for a house, reminiscent of woodmen's cottages in fairy tales. Living here you are wakened each morning at dawn by the singing of the birds; the volume of sound is tremendous, as each song echoes and re-echoes in the wood.

The lane goes straight on to Orgate, but opposite the cottage a field-path runs down the wood, across Marske Beck where there is an old water-wheel, and up to the old Reeth road, continuing along this to a cottage near the top of a hill, opposite which a stile leads to a field-path again, for Marrick.

There are many ways to Richmond. You can take them all in turn, and forget for a time the new road. The old road from Reeth has the exhilaration of a common about it. On the hill above it, just out of the village, some well-defined cultivation ridges indicate early occupation here. Two miles along the road, half-way between Marske and Richmond, a stile leads to a footpath which crosses the fields to Willance's Leap on the top of Whitcliffe Scar. In 1606, Robert Willance, a draper in Richmond, whose father, owning lead-mines, had become wealthy and bought the estate and Manor House at Clints, was out hunting when a fog came on; and, not realizing where he was, he galloped his horse to the edge of the ravine. The terrified animal took three leaps, and fell two hundred feet over the cliff. It was killed instantly, but Willance escaped with a broken leg. He managed to keep alive until help came by cutting open the horse, and laying his leg against the warm flesh. To commemorate his escape he caused three stones to be erected where the horse had taken the fatal leaps; on each is the inscription '1606. Glory be to our merciful God who miraculously preserved me from the danger so great.' Robert Willance was succeeded in his estates by his nephew Brian Willance, whose daughter married Dr. John Bathurst of Arkengarthdale, into whose hands the estate of Clints passed.

Beacon Hill, on the other side of the road, a little nearer to Richmond, 1,047 ft. above sea-level, is the highest point from Richmond to the sea coast, and was used for alarm signals in early days. In clear weather York Minster, forty miles to the south-east, the Cleveland Hills, the tower of Hartlepool church, and the country round the Tees estuary can be seen from it. The road enters Richmond by the old race-course.

Another way from Marske to Richmond lies along the field path to Applegarth, taking a stile on the right a little way up the old road. Here we would mention again the tendency of Swaledale farmers to leave bulls in fields which are crossed by public footpaths. We were once followed very suspiciously by a bull along this path to Applegarth, and, not wishing to be its first victims, we escaped into a farm kitchen to the astonishment of the mistress. The incident reminded the lady of how, in her childhood, a bull used to 'beeal' at her from a field high above the road as she went to school. 'Beeal' is a dialect word which comes from the Norse word *belja*, meaning to shout or cry out, and was in use in the district a thousand years ago.

The name of Applegarth came from the fact that, when all the land round was forest, a little tenement stood there with turf and fruit trees round it. A mansion followed this tenement which, with the estate, was granted by Earl FitzHugh of Ravensworth to Thomas Middleton for life. He kept a good establishment, having '11 horses and 12 milch kine. His silver plate in parlor was worth about £20.

His best suit of yellow satin worth £3,' etc. A description of the rather scanty furniture in the hall says, that in the same room were 'strange to say, a hanger or bench to put cheeses on, and a plate on which the family roasted the apples that grew in the orchard.' The owner of the farm-house which has replaced this mansion has some interesting paintings of it during the last century. The place is known as West Applegarth, and the farm lower down as East Applegarth.

On the low slopes of Whitcliffe Scar, a little beyond Applegarth, at the foot of Willance's Leap, is the site of an ancient British camp. There has been no attempt at excavation, and it is not easy to find, but the main dwelling area with two wings can be traced. A ditch runs round it, and there are two good examples of circular dwellings in the thickness of the wall. These had underground entrances, and would originally be roofed by branches covered with ling and turf. Charcoal has been found in them. There are east and west entrances to the camp, and a tumulus near the west one. York Museum has a grinding-stone which dates from about 4000 B.C., found on this site. This was formerly in Richmond Museum—now extinct, most of the specimens having gone to York and Hull.

From here the path goes through Whitcliffe Woods to the top of the hill, turning into a lane on its way to Richmond. From it there are fine views of the old town and its many towers, and you see how Richmond lies at the foot of the dale, rounding it off.

Another way to Richmond is to take the road or the field-path to Downholme Bridge, passing Marske Hall which looks across the road down a fine avenue of lime-trees; the road cuts through the hall grounds, dividing the house from much of the garden. It is thought that these limes were planted to make a new entrance to the hall, by diverting the road to the far side of the village, a scheme which was never carried out. Where Downholme Bridge joins the main road you turn to the right, and then to the left up the Leyburn road.

A little way up this road, Downholme church, protected by a row of fir-trees, stands alone, away from the village, as though watching both it and the high road. It is a compact church, on entering which it is easy to shut out the world. Nothing mars its restfulness. Sufficient for simple needs, it has also a beauty which uplifts and makes humdrum lives forgotten for a time. Originally built in the twelfth century, of that period only the south doorway with zigzag ornament, and a blocked north doorway remain. The north aisle and chancel arch, rebuilt in the Early English period, have 'nail-head' ornament. Walburn Hall, a fine Elizabethan manor house, stands about a mile beyond Downholme church on the Leyburn road.

The village itself lies up a smaller road to the left. Here there was once a stately hall of which only the vaulted cellars remain. It is said that an underground passage runs from them to Ellerton. An ivy-covered cottage which has been an inn has this inscription above the door: 'Good ale to-morrow for nothing. August 10 1694.'

From Downholme the road is an open highway across the moor, where it would not be surprising to meet the pedlars and carriers of a bygone day. Next it passes through Hudswell whose church was rebuilt during the nineteenth century. From a corner of the churchyard there is an unusual view of Richmond, resting sombre against the hillside, the smoke from its chimneys hanging over it in a gentle haze. Until about a century ago ravens nested on the scars below Hudswell. Down the sides of them an old jagger road from Leyburn went on its way to ford the river, took the easiest way up Whitcliffe Scar, and then ran near Beacon

Hill where traces of it can still be seen on its way to Durham. The ponies used for carrying in the pack-horse days were called jaggers, and the jagger roads were named after them. Along this one coal was brought from Durham into Wensleydale and beyond. A path still marks the track.

Passing a road which turns on the right down to Bellerby over Bellerby Moor, where one of the Huttons shot what was said to be the last wild deer in Swaledale, the highway comes to an old toll house. Here the road bends sharply to the left, and there is a sudden view of Richmond Castle below. This romantic way of entering Richmond was, until the beginning of the last century, the only way from the south.

And now there only remains the new road down the dale which the Marske road joins at Downholme Bridge. It, too, is a lovely way, running along a wooded hill-side with the river far below. At Downholme Park, the first house past the bridge, there is an ancient press, a wooden frame supporting a huge square stone, which was screwed down on to a grooved stone. This was no doubt built as a cheese-press, being of a type common up to a hundred years ago. But it is also known to have been used by the farmer two or three generations ago as a cider-press for making his own cider. The Downholme quarries farther on make an ugly gash on the face of the hill. Stone from them is carried up the dale for repairing the roads once kept by the farmers. Unfortunately, brick, not stone, has been used for recent building in Richmond.

The warning notices on this road are an unfailing source of interest. In startling succession they tell of landslides, road subsidences, the probability of falls of stone, and heavy lorries darting from the quarry; it would seem that our ancestors were wise to lay their road across the valley, for if it is hillier it is more solid and enduring. Through all these perils the road leads into Richmond, at the entrance to which are new brick and stucco houses, out of harmony with the weathered stone. Once in the town the road goes along by Grey Friar's tower to join another and with it run into the market-place.

Richmond Market-place

CHAPTER XVII

RICHMOND

RICHMOND with its market-place, its church with shops built into it, its castle, its cobble-stones, seems too good to be true. It is a place one has dreamed of, but not hoped to find. In its own way it is as satisfying as the fells. It does not unbend, a long, proud history has given gravity and dignity, but it spreads itself out for one to imagine what one will.

The name of Richmond, unlike most in the dale, was given to it by the Normans. It comes from the old French, *riche* and *mont*, and means a strong hill; there are many examples of the name in France. It is called Hindrelac in the 'Domesday Book.' Four hundred years after the Conquest, Richmond gave its name to Richmond on the banks of the Thames, both estates being owned at that time by the same earl.

The first town, round which Edward II, in 1312, gave the

Earl of Richmond permission to build a wall to keep out the raiding Scots, occupied the space of the market-place; it was really the outer bailey of the castle with which it had grown from the end of the eleventh century. There were three gates, 'Frenchgate, Finkelstreate Gate, and Bargate,' of which nothing now remains but their names in the streets.

There has been much written about the sacrilege of pulling down the old market cross in 1771. Probably built when the market charter of Henry VI was renewed in 1440, it was an enormous erection, enclosed by a wall six feet high, in which there were curious Gothic compartments. On the buttress at each corner was the figure of a sitting dog. A flight of steps led to a square platform on which was a massive pillar with an ornamental cross at the top. Butter and produce were sold within the walls, and religious meetings held. On the north-west exterior of this cross, criminals were tied to iron rings and flogged; the pillory stood near. Richmond's wheat, oat, and barley crosses, at which these corns were sold, have also vanished. But if the present cross has no architectural value, you become fond of the tall pillar crowned with a ball, and with steps all round it, on which the dales-people sit to wait for their buses.

Near it, in the centre of the market-place, is the conglomeration of Holy Trinity Church. No other church in England has shops built into its walls, and probably no other church has had such a chequered history and survived. Built about 1150, it had a period of importance, but soon became too small for the growing town, and the parish church was built outside the walls. In 1360 it was a ruin, and had to be rebuilt, but was again a ruin at the time of the Dissolution. It was used as a refuge during the plague which visited Richmond severely in 1597 and 1598; it has also been a school and a warehouse for beer and earthenware. In 1567 a charter of Queen Elizabeth provided that the building should be used for transacting the business of the town, and the north aisle was used as a town hall and a court for assizes. In 1745 it was restored as a church again, shops were built under the north aisle, the nave was shortened, thus cutting it off from the tower, and shops were built in between them. The south aisle had been pulled down previous to this, and built into cottages. During one of the restorations the wall-paintings mentioned by Leland as 'straung figures in the waulles of it. The people there dreme that it was (ons a temple of i) doles,' were covered up.

The shops are now removed from the tower, but those under the north aisle remain; the shape of the aisle steps can be seen on their ceilings. The tower is still separated from the church, and serves as a clock-tower for the town; from it the curfew is rung at eight o'clock by the bell placed there in the twelfth century. In 1888 Trinity Church was made the chapel of Richmond Grammar School. Through all its changes it has retained its Early English doorway with contemporary iron scroll-work.

The market-place is not the only cobbled way. Indeed, such roads seem unending. As Leland has it, 'Richemont is pavid.' Narrow alleys and wide streets run at all angles, with grass growing between the cobbles at the edges. The hill-sides are a network of them, some so narrow that the houses nearly touch each other at the top, some so steep that they are nothing but steps. Wandering up and down them the magic of the old town is revealed.

Newbiggin, a spacious road where footsteps seem suddenly muffled, turns off at the south-west corner of the market-place. Bargate, another broad way, runs down to Bargate Green and the old bridge. This road starts out influenced by the dignity of Newbiggin, but the houses get smaller as it descends, until, near the bottom, are what would be slums in a less artistic place. The view of the castle from Bargate Green, with the cottages clustering up to its walls, has the mystery and fascination of a foreign scene, a lethargy not typical of England.

The people sitting gossiping on their doorsteps, or hanging out clothes in the alleys, might be those Bretons who followed the Duke of Brittany to his new English lands. The old rhyme seems applicable to-day:

> Each came out of Brittany,
> With his wife Tiffany,
> And his maid Mangras,
> And his dog Hardigras.

There are not many days in the summer when an artist does not paint or draw the castle from Bargate Green. The same could almost be said of the view from across the river with the bridge in the foreground, which Turner painted.

The path along the river-side leads to the Round Howe, passing on the way a rift in the rock known as Arthur's Oven. A girl of whom we asked the way told us that was the oven in which Alfred burnt the cakes! The Howe is a round, isolated hill, topped with trees, and rising to a peak. The cliff from which it is cut off makes a kind of amphitheatre half-way round it. This is another example of the rush of water towards the end of the Ice Age overflowing the normal bed of the river, and cutting another channel through a fault in the strata. The new channel was also blocked later by deposit.

The Ice Age made a much greater change to the land on which Richmond town now stands. Before that period the river flowed on the north side of the market-place, and again the rush of water cut the way through the rock below the castle cliff. But deposit from shrinking glaciers filled in the old, not the new, bed.

Coming back along the river-path, the round turret on the hill to the left is Culloden Tower. It was erected on the site of an old castle, Hudswell Peele, to commemorate the victory of Culloden.

The hill beyond the bridge is another view-point for the castle. It is a good plan to turn up a field-path near some cottages on the right, and see it first from there, then follow the path on to the road, turn to the left, and again to the left at the toll house which was reached from Hudswell. From here, looking straight down on to the castle, you get a clear idea of its plan and the strength of its position, and see how it must have protected and dominated the town. And then, if not before, the desire comes to be inside those walls, exploring the ruins, learning its history, and imagining tales about it.

From Bargate, Cornforth Hill climbs up through an ancient gateway to Castle Wynd and the entrance, which was originally over a drawbridge across the moat. Here the great keep rises, massive and strong, as though it had been built but a generation, not seven centuries ago. Its walls are eleven feet thick and it is ninety-nine feet high, the loftiest tower-keep in England in relation to its base dimensions, though there are three others actually higher. Entering the gateway, wide, well-kept lawns, the inner bailey of the castle, stretch before you. An air of peace and stillness descends, and the days when it was in its full pride and glory seem not so far away.

This was the site so cleverly chosen by the Norman duke for a fortress to protect the vast estates given him by the Conqueror. Unlike most gifts of land at that time, the estate of Gillingshire was in a ring, so that, where many lords had to build ten or twelve castles to protect their lands, Earl Alan had only one. This is probably the reason why Richmond Castle, like Scarborough, was built in the first place of stone instead of wood and earth. Whether he chose the site unaided, or there was a garrison or camp there before

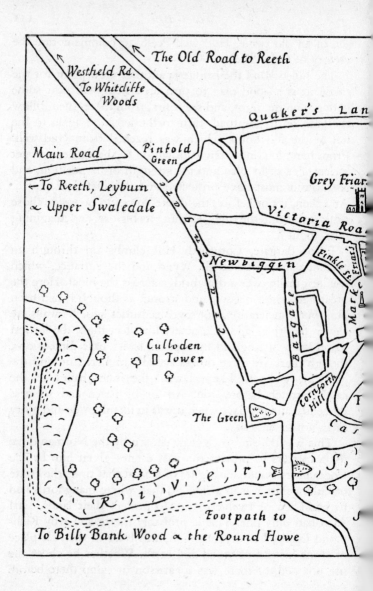

The Old Road to Reeth

Westheld Rd.
To Whitcliffe
Woods

Quaker's Lan

Main Road

Pinfold
Green

Grey Friar.

←To Reeth, Leyburn
∝ Upper Swaledale

Victoria Roa.

Newbiggin

Finkle St. Friars

Culloden
Tower

Bargate

Cornforth
Hill

The Green

Cas

R i v e r

S

Footpath to
To Billy Bank Wood ∝ the Round Howe

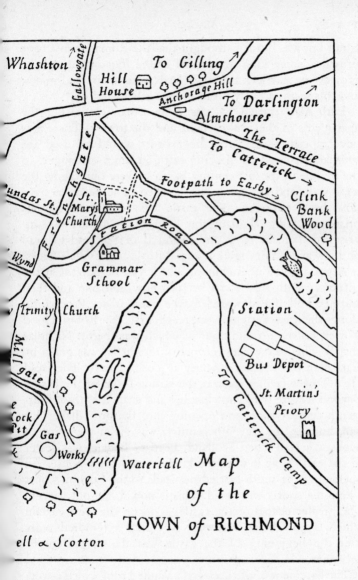

Whashton

Gallowgate

To Gilling

Hill House

Anchorage Hill

To Darlington
Almshouses

The Terrace

To Catterick →

Dundas St.

Frenchgate

St. Marys Church

Station Road

Footpath to Easby →

Clink Bank Wood

Wynd

Grammar School

Trinity Church

Station

Mill gate

Bus Depot

To Catterick Camp

St. Martin's Priory

Cock Pitt

Gas Works

Waterfall

Map of the
TOWN of RICHMOND

ell & Scotton

is not known, but it is thought that the Romans must have provided some kind of outpost at the foot of the dale to protect the carriers bringing lead from their lead-mines; and this seems a likely position for such a garrison.

Earl Alan started his castle immediately, putting the apartments in the wall-curtains and the towers. There was never a central hall; the inner court would be used for tournaments, and for grazing cattle in times of danger. In the middle of the last century barracks were built along the west wall, and the grass was levelled. The barracks have now been removed. The castle has had some famous prisoners. King William the Lion of Scotland was imprisoned there in 1174, and David II of Scotland in 1346 on his way to York after the fatal battle of Neville's Cross.

A good guide of Richmond Castle can be bought at the entrance. With this it can be seen how first one and then another building appeared as the need arose. Proceeding along the east curtain, you reach first the Robin Hood Tower, on the ground floor of which was the St. Nicholas chapel. This, the earliest chapel of the castle, was given by Earl Alan to St. Mary's Abbey at York in 1085. The Gold Hole Tower farther on was the strong-room of the castle. Beyond it were the great chamber and chapel, both of fourteenth century date, and opening into the great hall. This hall, built in the eleventh century, was given the name of Scolland's Hall when Scolland, Lord of Bedale, was sewer to the earl. Near it were the kitchens and brew-house. An opening at the south-east corner leads to the Cockpit Court where the sports were held. This is now a laid-out garden. The greater chapel of the castle stood on the west curtain which is now being restored. Not until a hundred years after the beginning of the castle was the keep thought necessary.

The basement of the keep has a vaulted roof which covers

the castle well. Above this are three stories, the top of which is open to the sky. The entrance is in the first story which, like the second, has one large room and chambers in the thickness of the wall. The stone stairway also runs between walls, an unusual feature for this date. It leads to the battlements of the third story. From here the Vale of Mowbray and the ruins of Easby Abbey can be seen to the north and east; the dale down which we have wandered to the west; and, immediately below, the busy life of the market-place.

In the spacious court where once the earls of Richmond lived their triumphs and disasters, you are reminded of the legends of Richmond Castle. Of King Arthur and his knights asleep somewhere beneath its walls, and one Potter Thompson who found the entrance to where they slept with the sword Excalibur and a jewelled horn on a table near. Of how the potter picked up these, but was frightened when he saw the knights move, and fled, hearing as he ran a voice saying:

> Potter, Potter Thompson
> If thou hadst either drawn
> The sword or blown the horn,
> Thou'd been the luckiest man
> That ever yet was born!

Legends too of underground passages to St. Martin's and Easby. Of the drummer boy who bravely started out to explore the one to Easby, beating his drum as he went, and of how listening soldiers followed the beat of the drum across the town, down the hill, and into the woods leading to Easby, till, at a place called Clink Bank, it stopped; and the drummer boy was never seen again. There were reasons for these legends springing up. In his plan of Richmond dated 1610, Speed shows an opening in Earl's Orchard, a level field across the river to the south of the castle, 'a vault that goeth under the River, and ascendeth up into the castell.'

The fate of Richmond Castle was not so violent as many. It was too far from main thoroughfares to play much part in history, and it was never besieged. Time, not war, brought about its ruin, a decay so slow that it did not feel the pain of it, nor lose its dignity.

At the far end of the market-place from the castle is a narrow passage known as Friar's Wynd. Many of the passages in Richmond have the name of 'wynd,' like those in Edinburgh; the name is found also in Darlington. Friar's Wynd leads to the monastery of Grey Friars, in the grounds of which was the only well besides that in the castle keep. The Franciscan friars allowed the towns-people to draw from the well in return for the use of the wynd. Part of the gateway through which they entered the town still remains. The Perpendicular tower, one of the most graceful in Yorkshire, seems lonely in its isolation. It is all that was completed of a new church at the time of the Dissolution. The Friary House, now the boarding-house of the grammar school, stands on the site of the friar's house.

Opposite Grey Friars, at the entrance to Friar's Wynd, is an almost perfect specimen of an eighteenth century theatre. It is now used as a furniture warehouse and auction room, and few people seem to know of its existence. There is the pay-box at the door, and a tiny dressing-room at the end of a passage. Two doors lead into the pit, down the sides of which there are seats and a barricade. The actors had to run up behind this barricade, in full view of the audience, from the dressing-room to the stage at the far end. The original gallery remains; it has a box at either end from which stairs led down to the stage. The theatre was said to hold people to the value of £40. In 1819 Edmund Kean played there. The bill announcing the event can be seen in a local tobacconist's.

Passing Grey Friars and turning in the direction from

which we entered the town, Victoria Road, after forking with Rosemary Lane, is joined on the right by Quaker Lane. At this junction a yard, now belonging to the corporation, marks the site of Pinfold Green, where sheep and cattle on their way to market were penned while the drovers rested.

The parish church of St. Mary's, on the hill down to the station, lost much of its character in the restoration of 1858, but two of its Norman arches are left at the west end of the nave. Its beautiful choir stalls were brought from Easby Abbey after the Dissolution. They have carved misericordes, one with a pig playing bagpipes while two little pigs dance. Over the mayor's stall is a shield from the abbey with the rebus of Abbot Bampton.

The church has an elaborate monument to the first Sir Timothy Hutton of Marske, who died in 1629, and his wife and children. Along the base are figures of the children, and appropriate verses. Under one child's name are the lines:

> As careful mothers do to sleeping lay
> Their babes, that would too long the wantons play,
> So to prevent my youth's approaching crimes
> Nature, my nurse, led me to bed betimes.

Under another of an infant in swaddling clothes, these:

> Into this world, as strangers to an inn,
> This infant came guest-wise, where when 't had been,
> And found no entertainment worth her stay,
> She only broke her fast and went away.

The old parish registers record the tremendous death-roll caused by the plague, of which ten hundred and fifty died in 1597-1598. Often twenty names are bracketed together, all having died in one day.

Richmond Grammar School is of very ancient foundation. It is known that there was a 'Gramer Schole kept within the towne of Richmond' in 1392. By the charter of Queen Elizabeth a new school was built in St. Mary's church-yard. The present building, erected in 1850 across the road from the church, is a memorial to the late Canon Tate, a great educationist, and headmaster of the school for thirty-seven years. Many famous men, among them Lewis Carroll, author of *Alice in Wonderland*, have been educated there.

The town can also lay claim to being the birthplace of Sir John Lawrence, the hero of Delhi, in 1811, to whose memory there is a monument in the church; of Henry Great-head, inventor of the lifeboat, in 1757; of Samuel Buck, an engraver, in 1696; and of George Cuitt, the famous etcher, in 1743.

Across the river, below St. Mary's, modern buildings dwarf the humble remains of St. Martin's Priory, the oldest religious institution in Richmond. Founded about 1100 as a cell for nine or ten monks attached to St. Mary's Abbey at York, it is now mixed up with farm buildings. There is a small Perpendicular tower, and, almost hidden by the wall of a barn, a fine Norman west doorway with zigzag mould-ing and scalloped capitals. It is probably the earliest example of architecture in the district.

The road running past St. Martin's was made by German prisoners during the war of 1914-18, and goes to Catterick Camp. From it the castle can be seen above Earl's Orchard, and the Castle Walk, a path cut round the cliff about the middle of the nineteenth century.

There were innumerable small religious houses in Rich-mond, the majority being chapels near the walls. Near Maison Dieu, at the junction of the Darlington and Catterick roads, the cell of a French anchoress was attached to the twelfth century chapel of St. Edmund. In 1618 this was con-verted into three almshouses, and given the name of the

Eleanor Bowes Hospital after the anchoress. A contemporary portrait of Queen Elizabeth, once in this building, is now in Richmond Town Hall. The end cottages have fine sepulchral carvings in the walls above the fireplaces. The blocked east window can be seen outside, though nearly covered by a garage. The buttresses on the east wall and the string-course with a band of medallions are part of the original chapel.

Frenchgate is another cobbled road. Some say it owes its name to the fact that the early Bretons who came over with succeeding Dukes of Brittany settled in that quarter. Centuries ago, when the roads were in very bad condition, men who owned estates higher up the dale had a 'town house' in Richmond to which they came for the winter. Robert Willance who took the famous leap over Whitcliffe Scar had a house there as well as his Manor House at Clints. Even to-day there is about Richmond the assured air of a capital. Frenchgate, its tall houses opening on to the road, might be a residential street near the centre of London.

At Hill House, near the top of Frenchgate, lived Fanny I'Anson, the lady of whom the song, *The Lass of Richmond Hill*, was written. This is often mistakenly thought to refer to Richmond in Surrey. Miss I'Anson married the author of the poem. Miss Millbank, who married Byron, also lived at Hill House.

Lying as it does, four miles from a great main road, Richmond has kept unspoilt its atmosphere of the past. Its people, influenced by tradition, have the same detached, leisurely air, and indifference to the rest of the world. Because a stranger never really belongs, Richmond is a place to visit often rather than to stay in long, taking away memories of it, and coming back to renew them.

Like an echo of the past there is a soldiers' camp again

near the town. Its coming has brought back some of the prosperity which had gone, especially to the shopkeepers. Many of the houses are occupied by its officers. It has brought back also the atmosphere of a garrison town, and the talk and trappings which go with it.

The Ruins of Easby Abbey

CHAPTER XVIII

EASBY

It is natural to follow on to Easby from Richmond. From various points in the town you can see its abbey ruins standing white and still in a curve of the river, as though they sought protection from the town, but must stay ever aloof from it. Seen at a distance, on moonlight nights their pale walls have the clarity and unearthliness of a mirage.

A path turns off below St. Mary's Church, and runs alongside the river to the abbey, first beside nursery gardens with acres of saplings, then through woods where the monks must surely have wandered meditating, or started out on fishing expeditions. Round a bend past the mill you come suddenly upon the ruins, in an open space, but sheltered by hills and trees; the kind of site which the monks or their patrons had a genius for choosing. In those days it was mostly woodland, and the monks cut down the trees and drained and cultivated the land. The path crosses the field above the ruins, and turns into the lane which leads to them.

The white-robed monks of Easby were great farmers, and did much of their own work. The cottage, its roof bent with age, where you pay sevenpence for admission to the abbey, was a granary attached to it. The monks used white horses and cattle, and in their white robes must have made a striking sight going about their work. On the green beyond the gatehouse, a mighty, gnarled elm-tree, with a hollow in its trunk large enough to hold several people, is called the 'Abbots' Elm,' because the abbots are said to have sat reading under it.

Easby Abbey was founded by Roald, Constable of Richmond Castle, in 1152, for Præmonstratensian monks, and was surrendered to Henry VIII's deputies in 1535. From that time until it was taken over by the Office of Works in 1930, it has slowly decayed; although in 1886 the Yorkshire Archæological Society raised a fund to excavate the ruins, and discovered the foundations of the church, and many of the infirmary buildings.

Approaching the frater, you enter over the site of the kitchen, the rougher stonework showing where it joined; a hole high in the wall was a hatch through which the food was pushed. The doorway now opens into cellars and store-houses, the vaulted roof of which supported the monk's frater or refectory. The beautiful Decorated east window with geometrical tracery, and six lofty windows along the south wall of the frater, remain; one, deeply recessed, was a pulpit from which a monk read aloud to the others during meals. It had a seat, and a pointed recess with crocketed hood-moulding was the aumbry or cupboard in which the book was kept. The abbot's aumbry was on the north wall. These monks were not allowed to speak among themselves, but in a little room under the frater they could talk occasionally to visitors.

From the vaults below the frater a door opens into the

cloister. This is irregular in shape, probably due to the fact that the monks, wishing to enlarge the abbey, altered their original plan, and did the best they could, hampered as they were by the river. This is also the reason why the whole range of building differs from the usual plan of a Cistercian monastery. The dorter ran along the west side. A small Norman doorway with a double row of beak-head carving opened to the stairs leading up to the dorter; it is all that remains of the first building. Beside it is a stone lavatory basin in which the monks would wash their hands on going up to or coming down from the dorter. The warming-room was under the north end of the dorter, and here the monks descending for the midnight service would warm themselves before proceeding to the church. Except for kitchen fires, and a later fireplace in the abbot's room, this seems to have been the only heated place in the monastery. Those early monks must have looked forward to the summer as the time in which they really lived; in winter their minds and bodies would surely be numbed by the cold.

Still, if there were few fires, there were no draughts, for all the doors were made to shut against a frame, and had raised and chamfered thresholds; and in those days the cloister would be shut in on all four sides. Now, at the north end, except for fragments of the chancel and the north and south transepts, only the foundations of the church remain. These, however, give a good idea of the plan, which was cruciform with an aisleless chancel, and a nave of seven bays with north and south aisles and transepts, each of which had an east aisle containing three chapels.

Several tomb-slabs incised with crosses fleury and a chalice, shears, or book have been discovered on the floor of the chapel; some have incised figures. Along the north wall of the choir are two recesses, thought to be the tombs of Roald, the founder, and his wife, Gracina. Here also many of the Scrope family, who afterwards owned the abbey and rebuilt much of it, were buried, Henry le Scrope in 1336 and Sir William le Scrope in 1344 being two of them.

Beyond the church are the infirmary buildings, some of the most complete of their kind known. A dormitory, hall, cellar, and chapel were connected with them; a window from the dormitory had a view of the altar in the chapel. The monks spent a few days in the infirmary after being bled, though the actual operation, which was done periodically, took place in a small room on a passage leading from the infirmary wing to the church. Only while in the infirmary were the monks allowed to eat meat.

The buildings on the east of the cloister were the sacristy, and the vaulted Early English chapter house, where business was transacted and the processionals formed. The quarters for guests were to the south-west of the abbey. The exterior wall of this section has a lovely, intersecting arcade, two of whose arches are pierced for windows.

Comparatively little is left of what must have been a very important establishment. But with what there is and what is known to have been, the monastery grows again in the imagination; the fine church rises up in the middle to dominate the rest, and the white-robed monks pace with bent heads through the cloisters. Its peace and serenity descend upon you, and something of the power and influence which the ancient walls implied. You feel the charity of the priests, their conviction and their zeal, but you feel too their dominance.

There is a story of a dispute between the abbots and a family named Eglisclive over the ownership of two hundred and twenty acres of moor in Barden. The dispute lasted during the time of five abbots, until, in 1311, the abbots got into their possession a charter which they said proved them the owners. Robert de Eglisclive, frightened by threats of excommunication, confessed his guilt in keeping back the land, and received absolution. Then, being anxious for the souls of his father and grandfather who had also retained the land, he begged the abbots to pronounce absolution over their graves; after which he gave back the moor to them, sure of the safety of his own and his ancestors' souls. There was some uncertainty about the boundary line of this land, so the abbots placed stones where they considered it should be, caused Eglisclive to draw a furrow with a plough between them, and settled the matter. Their word was law, and few people were powerful enough to oppose them.

The river flows beside the abbey, and following it you see the town of Richmond lying grimly on the hill-side, its keep towering above as though to assure the abbey of its protection. A gentle choir of birds trills from the trees around, echoes of those choirs of saintly men. Then something alien creeps into the scene, a bright red bus descending the new road from Catterick Camp to Richmond. The present comes back with its troubles, its ugliness and selfishness, but with its beauty and enlightenment too; so that it is good to be standing weaving stories amongst the ruins rather than starting out from them after a night's lodging, in terror of the dangers of the way.

The windows of Easby Hall on the slope behind the abbey gaze for ever on this lovely scene with the gatehouse, still almost perfect, in the foreground. The road passed through the building, under curious arches which have a circular lower order and a pointed upper one. The lower story is late twelfth century, and the upper, once the abbot's court room, is of the Decorated period.

Close to the ruins, its unimposing exterior looking as though it were a part of them, stands the parish church of

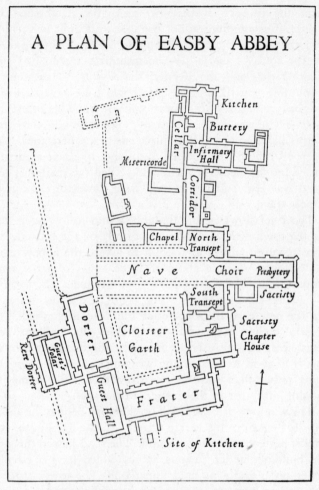

A PLAN OF EASBY ABBEY

Kitchen

Buttery

Cellar

Infirmary Hall

Misericorde

Corridor

Chapel

North Transept

Nave   Choir   Presbytery

Sacristy

South Transept

Dorter

Sacristy

Chapter House

Cloister Garth

Guest Solar

Rere Dorter

Guest Hall

Frater

Site of Kitchen

*This sketch-plan reproduced by permission of
H.M. Office of Works from measured plan.*

Easby, a solitary instance of a church enclosed in the precincts of a monastery. But Easby church was standing before ever the monks came. It saw the monastery slowly grow beside it, itself serving as the abbey church until the monks had built their own. For centuries it watched their placid life, until at last disquieting rumours and orders filled the air, and the gracious buildings were deserted, plundered, and fell into decay. For a few more centuries it watched the walls slowly crumble, till a more enlightened age with a new pride in its ancient buildings stopped the decay. To-day it sees other, vastly different crowds come down the lane to the abbey. They wander about the ruins, speculating over this and that, guessing, often wrongly. And the old church knows the answer to their guesses; it has seen those ruins as a home, a shelter, a sanctuary.

The church, like the abbey, is dedicated to St. Agatha, the persecuted saint of Sicily, probably because the Earl of Richmond or his constable, the founder, brought back some relics of this saint from the Second Crusade in 1146. The little church with its bell-turret is overshadowed by the abbey on its exterior, but it is full of interest. On entering it, attention is first caught by the elaborately carved early Norman font, dating from about 1100, at the west end. Then the twelfth century pillars and arches of the arcade covered with thirteenth century paintings give suddenly to the whole interior an almost barbaric beauty. Other paintings which have only recently been discovered on the south wall are also thirteenth century, but more modern texts have been painted over them. From them you pass to the marvellous frescoes in the chancel for which the church is famous. Covering both walls, these depict the Fall of Man and his Redemption by Christ. Those on the north side show Adam and then Eve in the Garden of Eden, their fall and expulsion to till the ground. Those on the south side show the Annunciation, the Birth of Christ, the Adoration of the Shepherds and the Magi, the Descent from the Cross, the Burial, and the Resurrection. There are also paintings of bishops in the sedilia, and representations of spring and winter in the north window recess. The frescoes have been restored, but many of the figures still retain their first spontaneity and naïve charm.

Under the north chancel wall is a plaster cast of a Northumbrian cross, the original of which is now in the Victoria and Albert Museum. Part of the shaft had been for a long time in the grounds of Easby Hall, and when its value was discovered it was sold to the museum. Then two pieces of carving built into the walls of the church, which had always been considered Saxon work, were seen to be remarkably like the sides of the cross. These were taken out and cleaned; and it was discovered that not only were they the sides, but complete pieces of the shaft which had been built sideways into the wall. These too were sold to the museum. The front represents Christ sitting in majesty with the disciples grouped below Him; the back has carvings of birds and animals. It seems a pity not to have the original cross there instead of a cast.

Still the treasures and relics of Easby crowd upon you: the fine piscina and sedilia in the chancel, the east window and windows in the aisle, the arch into the chapel, all of the Early English period when the church was enlarged and rebuilt. Part of the money which was obtained from the sale of the cross was used to buy curtains and altar hangings in the Early English style. To the east of the doorway is a holy water stoop cut out of a solid piece of stone; and on the other side a twisting stone staircase leads up to a priest's chamber, now used as a vestry. A narrow slit in its east wall looks over the south aisle to the altar. From outside you can see how this room is really an upper story of the porch. These rooms were often occupied by a priest or a person of high rank who, in his declining years, wished to enjoy religious privileges without having to journey to the church. The porch has a very large aumbry, and deep stone seats on either side. Here the business of the parish was transacted. Both the inner and outer doorways are Early English.

In 1790 there was discovered between the double oak boards used for cutting the communion bread on at Easby an epitaph, written in 1538, upon the death of Richard Swale, gentleman, extolling his virtues and gifts to the poor, 'after that he had lyved fourescore and sixe yeares one moneth and sixtene daies.' The epitaph is in verse, and is thought from its style to have been written by Miles Coverdale.

So you leave Easby to its memories, and climb up the lane to the cottages and the rather forsaken-looking almshouses at the top, which are all there is of a village. The road to the right goes to Catterick Bridge, that to the left turns back to Richmond. Beside this are stately houses, one of which is built over St. Nicholas Hospital, a resting-place for travellers connected with the abbey.

And then you are on the Terrace, lingering for its enchanting view of Richmond; the cottages crowding up to the castle walls, and the towers of Grey Friars and the two churches leading naturally up to the loftier keep. There is that feeling of unreality about it which is felt in the market-place, as though its spirit was in a past which has gone for ever.

In the market-place, the buses from Darlington and Catterick and Leyburn come, and go again; and those smaller ones which journey up the dale stand jauntily beside them. There in a corner is the little one which goes to Keld.

How it draws you, remembering those wind-swept villages and the friendly people in them. If only because the road up the dale leads out of it, there would be magic in the name of Richmond. And what greater praise can you give the old town than that it is a fitting end to Swaledale?

INDEX

171

LIST OF BOOKS CONSULTED

Itinerary, Leland (1535–46)
History of Richmond, Clarkson (1821)
History of Richmondshire, Whitaker (1823)
Romantic Richmondshire, H. Speight (1897)
Regal Richmond, E. Bogg (1909)
The Wild Borderland of Richmondshire, E. Bogg (1909)
The Place-Names of the North Riding, A. H. Smith
Memoirs of the Geological Survey, Mallerstang
Transactions of the Newcomen Society (Vol. VII), A. Raistrick
Yorkshire Archæological Society (Vol. VI, 'Marske'), Canon Raine
Victoria County History